To Grandma Anne

you've got a wonderful
grandson
Love + Peace
Martin Smith

Revolutionary Portraits

Frank Sinatra

WHEN OL' BLUE EYES WAS A RED

Martin Smith

REVOLUTIONARY PORTRAIT 7

Frank Sinatra – when Ol' Blue Eyes was a red by Martin Smith

Published June 2005 by

REDWORDS

1 Bloomsbury Street, London WC1B 3QE

www.redwords.org.uk

ISBN: 1 905192 02 9

Design and production: Roger Huddle and Hannah Dee

Printed by Bath Press

Redwords is linked to Bookmarks, the socialist bookshop

www.bookmarks.uk.com

This book is in the series **Revolutionary Portraits** from Redwords. The unifying theme in this eclectic collection is the relationship between individual artists and larger historical forces, how each influences and shapes the other. All of the books in this series aim to lead us back to these works of art and music with new eyes and ears, and a deeper understanding of how art can raise the human spirit.

Redwords is a publishing collective specialising in art, history and literature from a socialist perspective.
We are linked to Bookmarks, the socialist bookshop.

contents

Acknowledgements

A couple of summers ago I gave a talk on Frank Sinatra at an event in London called Marxism 2003. An elderly gentleman, who I had not met before and have not seen since, approached me and asked for my address. He said he wanted to send something to me. Two weeks later a parcel arrived containing an original 78rpm recording of Frank Sinatra's 'The House I Live In'. Inside was a small piece of paper with just two words on it – 'From George'. I have no way of contacting that kind man, but I would very much like to take this opportunity to thank him for the wonderful gift.

I would love to claim that I thought of the title of this book, but alas that is not the case. That honour goes to Jon Wiener and his pathbreaking essay, 'When Old Blue Eyes Was "Red"'.

In writing this book I have been helped enormously by the advice and comments of Chris Bambery, Michael Bradley, Hannah Dee and Lindsey German. Special thanks go to Judith Orr, whose suggestions, ideas and criticisms I truly value. Last but not least I would like to thank Roger Huddle, without whose encouragement this project would never have got off the ground.

This book is dedicated to Eve and Jim Smith.

You can contact the author at martinsmith27@hotmail.com

01 / I've got you under my skin

I grew up to the sound of Frank Sinatra. It wasn't a conscious decision. I suspect my childhood was like many others – Sinatra and his music were always around. I would wake up on a Sunday morning and Sinatra would be blasting out from our big wooden gramophone player. It was the same at weddings and parties. As the night wore on his records would be lovingly taken out of their sleeves and played. That was the signal for the party to begin. I remember drunken nights when uncles and aunts lost all their inhibitions, and dads danced like only dads can.

It is worth recalling that, before The Beatles and even before Elvis Presley, Frank Sinatra was the first pop superstar. In the 1940s young women fainted and swooned at his concerts, and young men copied the Sinatra look – even Donald Duck dressed like Frank! His was a career that spanned almost 60 years and would take his young fans on an incredible musical journey – a tour which guided them through adolescence and on into marriage and middle age, and ended in the autumn of their years. Many more fans joined along the way. Sinatra recorded over 80 albums and made more than 60 films.[1] His vocal style obviously influenced the likes of Dean Martin and Tony Bennett. But it also inspired singers as diverse as Marvin Gaye, Bono and even Robbie Williams.

Then there was the voice – that warm, lush baritone. It is a voice that has moved millions. Sinatra did not sing standards, he made them. I defy anyone to listen to the song 'I've Got You Under My Skin' and not feel glad to be alive. I challenge anyone to listen to the song 'In The Wee Small Hours Of The Morning' and not remember a love lost. If after listening to those records you ain't feeling it, then all I can say is, you ain't lived it.

One of Sinatra's greatest talents was his ability to extract real meaning from popular songs and unlock the emotions within us. For example, in 1963 Sinatra performed a benefit concert for the Civil Rights Movement at the prestigious Carnegie Hall in New York. Sitting in the balcony was Martin Luther King. One of the songs Sinatra performed that night was 'Ol' Man River'. It begins:

Here we all work long the Mississippi
Here we all work while the white folk play
Pulling them boats from the dawn till sunset
Getting no rest till the judgement day.

As Sinatra sang that gut-wrenching song about slavery, tears rolled down the cheeks of the great civil rights leader's face.[2]

One of the aims of this book is to celebrate Sinatra's contribution to modern music, and place it in some kind of political and historical context. But there is another reason for writing it. Today, many remember Sinatra as an entertainer who embraced Ronald Reagan, who loved to hang out with mobsters, and who used and abused those around him. Sinatra was all those things, I'm afraid, and worse. It is a side of Sinatra that should not be ignored.

But there was another Frank Sinatra, a radical Frank, who has been buried by the sands of time. At the height of his popularity in the 1940s, Sinatra was branded a 'Red'. He was one of the first major stars of the era to stand shoulder to shoulder with the poor and oppressed. Like Pablo Picasso, John Steinbeck, Billie Holiday and Charlie Chaplin, Sinatra was prepared to use his art to challenge the status quo. In 1946, a reporter asked Sinatra what he thought was the biggest problem America faced. He replied, 'Poverty. That's the biggest thorn…every kid in the world should have his quart of milk a day'.[3]

Sinatra was also a dedicated campaigner against racism. The great bandleader Duke Ellington remembered the singer as a person who 'led the campaign against racial intolerance in the 1940s'.[4] What inspired Sinatra to make that stand, and why did he sell out in later years? These are questions worth answering.

02 / You make me feel so young: the early years

If you stand on the western shores of Manhattan, New York, and look across the Hudson River you can see the city of Hoboken, New Jersey, the birthplace of Sinatra. This city of 70,000 was built on immigration. From 1880 to the beginning of the First World War more than 24 million people crossed the Atlantic from Europe. About 4.5 million came from Italy – the largest of any national group. About 80 percent of them were from the exhausted hills of the Mezzogiorno – the south and Sicily.[1]

Between 1860 and 1914 New York grew from a population of 850,000 to 4 million, Chicago from 110,000 to 2 million and Philadelphia from 650,000 to 1.5 million.[2] American industry expanded rapidly. Between 1880 and 1914, steel production rose by 250 percent and coal output increased from 14 million tons a year to more than 100 million tons. The American ruling class encouraged workers to come to toil on the land, in the mills and factories. Working class people were promised freedom and a land of opportunity. But the immigrants found themselves herded into overcrowded ghettoes, and the only choice they really had was to sell their labour power to one employer or another, or to fall into poverty.

In the 1890s, Sinatra's grandparents and their children made their separate passages from Italy. They settled in Hoboken, a city divided along ethnic lines. The Germans had been the first to arrive. They were well-off merchants who built their mansions high on the hill of Castle Point. The Irish came next. They made their homes in the middle of the town, and soon controlled the police and fire departments. The last to settle in the city were the Italians, who lived on the west side of town and were packed into five-storey wooden tenements. This area was known as Little Italy.

Sinatra's grandparents not only suffered the indignities of poverty, they also faced racial discrimination. Italians were barred from German and Irish clubs and churches, and denied access to the best jobs. In several interviews Sinatra discussed the racism he had faced as a child in Hoboken. He recalled, 'I was often called a Wop and chased and beaten by gangs from other neighbourhoods.' It was the US immigration authorities which coined the word 'Wop'. When Italian immigrants arrived at Ellis Island in New York, many came without papers. Immigration officers recorded this by stamping their entry visas WOP, and the abbreviation became a term of derision.

Italians even faced the horror of the lynch mob. In New Orleans in 1891 a group of 11 Italian immigrants were accused of murdering a corrupt police superintendent named David Hennessy. In the run-up to the trial, the press resorted to all kinds of racial stereotypes and prejudice, and wrote about the Black Hand, a secret gang of Italian criminals. However, a jury acquitted eight of the men and reached no verdict on the other three. Two days after the verdicts, while the 11 waited in custody for their release papers, a mob of several thousand stormed the jail and lynched or shot all 11 men. It remains the worst single case of lynching in US history.

This background had a profound effect on Sinatra and made him a committed anti-racist. He regularly donated money to the National Association for the Advancement of Coloured People (NAACP), one of the first organisations in the US to fight for black civil rights. Later in his life, Sinatra was asked why. His response is illuminating: 'When I was young, people used to ask me why I sent money to the NAACP and, you know, I tried to help in my own small way. I used to say, because we've been there too, man. It wasn't only black people hanging from the ends of those fucking ropes'.[3]

Of course, the vast majority of lynchings were of black people. An official study of vigilante killings revealed the shocking statistic that, on average, a black man was murdered each month in the US throughout the 1930s.[4]

A fresh injustice rocked the Italian American community in 1927 – the execution of two Italian-born anarchists,

Nicola Sacco and Bartolomeo Vanzetti. They were executed for supposedly murdering a clerk and a guard at a shoe factory in Braintree, Massachusetts. The evidence against them was circumstantial and, at the trial, the prosecution had concentrated on the pair's political beliefs, their immigrant status and the fact that they had refused to register for military service.

It is little wonder that many Italians did not feel welcome in America. The Italian community in Hoboken was closed off from the outside world. Few dared venture out of Little Italy. Most could not speak English and feared the police, who circulated rumours that they had the power to deport people or, worse, send them back to Ellis Island. Partly as a response, the Italian community in Hoboken carved out its own community organisations, churches, trade unions and gangs.

On Valentine's Day 1914 Natalie Della Garavante (everyone called her Dolly) married Anthony Martin Sinatra (Marty) in the City Hall in Jersey City. They rented an apartment in the heart of Little Italy, and on 15 December 1915 Francis Albert Sinatra was born. By all accounts, Marty Sinatra was a shy, retiring man. Originally from Sicily, he spent his younger years in Hoboken working at a wide range of jobs – some legal and others not. He was a professional boxer for a while, fighting under the name of Marty O'Brien. In the early 20th century Italian boxers often used Irish names to win acceptance from a wider public.

Dolly was also an immigrant, from northern Italy. She was the opposite of Marty, a strong and forceful woman who had high hopes for herself and her family. Dolly spoke perfect

English, as well as all the dialects of Little Italy. Many of her neighbours turned to her for help in filling in forms and dealing with the authorities. She was also the person in Little Italy to whom the Irish politicians could go when they needed Italian votes. She became the Democratic leader of the third ward in the ninth district of Hoboken, a position not held before by either an Italian or a woman. Dolly created a power base that could deliver 600 votes for the Democratic Party. It was a kind of politics that had nothing to do with beliefs and everything to do with patronage.

Dolly also became a midwife and was prepared to perform abortions, which made her popular with the young women and families she helped, but pitted her against the local Catholic church. Dolly was arrested and prosecuted several times, but her political connections meant she never went to jail.

Sinatra remembered, 'My mother is what you would call a progressive… She was always interested in conditions outside her own home. My father too, but he was the more silent type'.[5] From an early age Frank Sinatra helped carry placards for the Democratic Party.[6]

Hoboken's world was turned upside down on 2 April 1917 when the US entered the First World War against Germany. Hoboken became a major port of embarkation for US troops going to fight in Europe. The balance of forces in the city quickly changed. The German population was ostracised and driven out. The Irish now controlled the city, despite the fact that more and more Italians were moving in. Dolly was summoned to the mayor's office where, in addition to her duties as a ward leader, she became the official interpreter to the municipal court and was paid to accompany immigrants when they appeared before a judge. She used her political connections to get jobs for the family, and Marty was appointed to the Hoboken fire department.

But it was an event a few years later which transformed the fortunes of Sinatra's family. At the stroke of midnight on 16 January 1920 America went dry. For the next 13 years, Prohibition made it illegal to buy or sell alcohol. Yet rather than discourage drinking and partying, this had the opposite effect. Thousands of illegal drinking dens and nightclubs opened. The 'Roaring Twenties' had begun.

Prohibition proved a bonanza for Italian, Irish and Jewish gangsters who came to control the supply and distribution of alcohol. Hoboken became an entry point for shipments of foreign liquor, and bars sprang up everywhere. With the local administration failing to enforce the law, 250 bars were established in a square mile of the city.[7] The Sinatras ran their own bar, called Marty O'Brien's.

By the time Frank turned 12, Dolly and Marty could afford to move out of Little Italy. They found a three-bedroom apartment at 703 Park Avenue in the German-Irish neighbourhood. It was only ten blocks from their former tenement building, but to their old neighbours in Little Italy it felt like a million miles away. The Sinatras were moving up in the world.

Frank was no poor kid from the block. According to many childhood friends his mother lavished him with clothes and toys. But that did not mean he could escape the injustices of racism and gang violence. Italian gangs would fight the Irish and vice versa. Sinatra later argued that these experiences made him a champion of racial equality. He told one magazine that, when he was a child playing in the undergrowth near the Hudson River, he and his friends came upon a Ku Klux Klan meeting. They ran home to tell their fathers, who rushed the bigots with baseball bats.[8]

Music was an important part of his life. Dolly sang at parties and political rallies, Frank sang in a church choir and in his parents' bar. The radio was an especially important influence in his teenage years. The formation of national broadcasters NBC in 1927 and CBS in 1928 offered audiences round the clock, coast to coast music. Dolly bought Frank a radio. But it wasn't like everybody else's in Frank's neighbourhood – it was the size of a grand piano. The young Sinatra grew up listening to the stars of the day, such as Fred Astaire, Rudy Vallee, Russ Columbo and his all time favourite, Bing Crosby.

Crosby was one of the most successful recording artists of the 20th century. He recorded over 2,500 songs and sold more than 250 million records. His crooning style represented a decisive shift in singing. In contrast to earlier singers – who sang with a precise, often stilted diction and phrasing – Crosby introduced a loose, more relaxed approach. This style was made possible by the introduction of electronic recording techniques, which meant the vocalist could put more emphasis on expression and range rather than having to concentrate on being audible.

The Roaring Twenties ended in the stockmarket crash of 1929, which marked the beginning of the Great Depression.

There had never been a slump that went so deep or lasted so long. Millions of people's lives were turned upside down. Poverty and unemployment stalked the world. In the US, industrial output fell by 46 percent. Up to 15 million US workers lost their jobs, and the wages of those in work fell by 39 percent. There were unemployment riots and marches all over the country. Veterans of the First World War camped outside the White House demanding the payment of money owed to them. Amid the desperation, the election in 1932 of a Democratic president, Franklin D Roosevelt, appeared to offer a glimmer of hope.

America's rulers had become desperate to get the economy moving and were willing to implement radical measures. Roosevelt pushed through a programme of reform legislation which became known as the 'New Deal'. The government introduced the National Recovery Act, designed to take control of the economy by fixing wages and prices, and limiting competition. Unemployed workers were put to work on massive building projects, and the administration tried to reorganise agricultural production. Some measures even made it easier for workers to form unions.

The New Deal aimed to stabilise the economy and stop the lower classes from rebelling. As historian Howard Zinn notes, 'The Roosevelt reforms went far beyond previous legislation. They had to meet two pressing needs: to reorganise capitalism in such a way as to overcome the crisis and stabilise the system; and head off the alarming growth of spontaneous rebellion in the early years of the Roosevelt administration'.[9]

Compared with the previous administration, which used troops to smash marches by the unemployed, Roosevelt's administration seemed positively left wing. But Roosevelt was no socialist. The Democratic Party to which he belonged had been the party of the slave owners in the 19th century. By the 1930s it represented a coalition between Southern segregationists and key sections of the ruling class. Roosevelt was by no means as radical as is often suggested. Rather than use government spending to end the crisis, he cut veterans' pensions and remained committed to a balanced budget.

But the working class and the poor did not simply wait for the government to act. They created unemployed councils to fight for jobs, and tenants' committees to fight evictions. City-wide general strikes and sit-down protests rocked the bosses. These struggles had a major impact on Sinatra's view of the world, and one of the key organisations behind them was the US Communist Party (CPUSA) – but more of it later.

Financially, the depression did not affect Sinatra. Having a father with a steady job and a mother with several meant he escaped the ravages of the worst economic disaster the country had known. In fact, life improved for the Sinatras. The family moved into a four-storey wooden house in Hoboken, which cost $13,400 – a huge amount of money at the time.

By 1935, Frank was 20 years old and still living at home. He was without a steady job, although he did some casual work in the local shipyards. But being a star was all he cared about. He started out singing at parties and weddings. As the

1930s wore on, a new form of jazz developed. The depression had not ended, but young Americans were ready for a music that offered hope and celebrated having fun – the era of swing had begun. Band leaders such as Count Basie, Benny Goodman, Artie Shaw, Tommy Dorsey and Duke Ellington became household names. Swing had a massive influence on music, and was popular among black and white audiences. At the time, the musicians were the main attraction and the vocalist was an added extra, although there were exceptions – Bing Crosby, Fred Astaire and Al Jolson were famous singers in their own right.

Frank's mother got him his first big break as a singer in 1935 in a vocal group called The Three Flames. With the addition of Frank, they became The Hoboken Four. In the same year, the group joined a tour organised by promoter Major Bowes. Part of the show involved Frank blacking his face to play the part of a minstrel – a hangover from a 19th century celebration of white power.

In February 1939, Frank married a young local woman, Nancy Barbatos, with whom he would have three children – Nancy, Franklin (named after President Roosevelt) and Tina. In the same year, Sinatra joined the Harry James Band, an up and coming swing band. In order to get gigs, there was pressure on Frank to hide his Italian roots. But it was something he would never do. Years later, Sinatra recalled, 'I was just another American kid. Then I discovered at what? Five? Six? I discovered that some people thought I was a Dago, a Wop, a Guinea. That's why years later, when Harry [James] wanted me to change my name, I said no way, baby. The name is Sinatra. Frank fucking Sinatra'.[10]

Sinatra was hungry for fame and fortune, but did not think he would achieve it in the Harry James Band. His big break came when he joined Tommy Dorsey in January 1940. The Tommy Dorsey Band was one of the most successful swing-era big bands. Throughout the 1930s and 1940s Dorsey assembled some great musicians and singers – Buddy Rich (drums), Bunny Berigan (trumpet), Jo Stafford (vocals) and Connie Haines (vocals). The song that launched Sinatra's career was 'I'll Never Smile Again'. It stayed at the number one spot for weeks.

Frank singing with Tommy Dorsey, 1940

After that, Tommy put Frank's name above those of all the other band members.

Frank took his singing very seriously: 'I began listening to musicians both jazz and classical, for instance I was fascinated by [violinist] Jascha Heifetz, who could make a change of his bow in phrase and get to the end of the bow and continue without a perceptible missing beat in the motion. I thought if that could be done on an instrument…why not do it with the human voice? It was very tough to do it. It took a lot of calisthenics and physical work to get the bellows – the breathing apparatus built up'.[11] Sinatra was not really a jazz singer in the conventional way. His vocal style was influenced by jazz, but had its roots in other musical genres – popular song, concert music and the bel canto style of Italian opera singing.

Dorsey's perfect legato trombone style and high tone

influenced Sinatra heavily. In essence, Dorsey sang with his trombone. Sinatra copied the mouth control and breathing technique of the trombone player and bandleader, which allowed him to breathe while singing.

Another person who had a profound impact on Sinatra

was Billie Holiday. Sinatra regularly attended her gigs and sent her money during hard times. He studied her voice and phrasing. When Holiday was asked what impact she thought she'd had on Sinatra's vocal technique, she said, 'Bending those notes, that's all I helped him with.' But her modesty belies the fact that she was as responsible as anyone for the Sinatra sound.

Billie Holiday in full flight

The earliest stories about Sinatra's hatred of racism date from his days as a singer with Tommy Dorsey. Sy Oliver, an Afro-American, was Dorsey's arranger. Sinatra offered to share a hotel room with him on tour. When a hotel clerk refused to allow Oliver to stay in a whites-only hotel, Sinatra was outraged. He pulled the clerk across the counter and threatened to smash up the hotel if the man did not give Oliver a key immediately. The clerk had a change of heart.[12]

It was as part of the Tommy Dorsey Band that Sinatra became a major star. In 1941 he was named top band vocalist by *Billboard* magazine and, by the end of the year, had displaced his idol Bing Crosby at the top of *Downbeat* magazine's poll – a position Crosby had held for six years.

In January 1942, Dorsey agreed to let Frank record as a

solo artist. Axel Stordahl was arranger and conductor for the date. They recorded four tracks – 'Night and Day', 'The Night We Called it a Day', 'The Song is You' and 'Lamplighters Serenade'. Shortly after recording the tracks Sinatra played them to the other members of Dorsey's band. Connie Haines takes up the story: 'They put that record on the loudspeaker, and Frank's voice began to fill the Palladium. We all knew it was a hit. Frank knew it too, because he said, "Hey, Bing, old man. Move over, here I come".'[13]

03 / It all came true: the bobbysox years

Frank Sinatra made his solo debut on 30 December 1942 at one of the shrines of the swing era – the New York Paramount Theatre. It was a four-week booking and Frank was bottom of the bill. He was supporting Benny Goodman, the King of Swing, the country's number one bandleader.

What happened on the first night has entered music folklore. For an hour Benny Goodman dazzled the audience with his music before announcing, 'And now Frank Sinatra.' Frank stuck his head and one foot through the curtains and froze. Immediately, the girls in the audience let out a deafening scream. Goodman exclaimed, 'What the fuck was that?' Sinatra laughed, ran up to the microphone and sang 'For Me And My Gal'. Pandemonium broke out.

Sinatra and the Tommy Dorsey Band were now history.

There were contractual problems, of course, but they were sorted out – one way or another. A few days after the first Paramount concert, publicist George Evans attended one of Sinatra's shows. He saw the impact Frank had on the young, mainly female audience, and acted quickly to become Sinatra's press agent and set about making him a star. Evans told a few, select press columnists of a new singer who was going to be bigger than Bing Crosby, and invited them to one of Sinatra's shows. He hired 12 girls for the occasion to swoon and pass out when Sinatra walked on stage. But he needn't have bothered – 30 fainted spontaneously and had to be carried out of the auditorium.

For the next four weeks the Paramount was packed. When the booking finished, the theatre signed Sinatra for another four weeks, this time with star billing. The hysteria at the concerts reached fever pitch, with teenagers screaming and fainting, and a few excitable souls throwing their bras on stage. This was the era of the 'bobbysoxers', and Frank was their number one guy. The term came from the clothes these teenage girls wore – white ankle socks, worn with white or brown loafers or sandals, pleated skirts and pastel coloured sweaters.

George Evans christened his new client 'The Voice', and set about rewriting Frank's past. Evans took two years off Sinatra's age, claiming he was born in 1917 rather than 1915, to make Frank a bit closer to the age of his fans. He depicted Frank as a child of the Depression who knew only poverty and deprivation. The boy who had hated athletics at school was turned into a sporting legend – a kind of white Paul

Robeson. Frank was supposed to have played American football like a 240-pound beefcake, run around a sports track like Jesse Owens and dunked a basketball like one of the Harlem Globetrotters. Sinatra's immigrant parents became native-born Americans, and Dolly, the Hoboken midwife, became a Red Cross nurse who had served her country in the First World War. Overnight, Frank was the American dream personified.

Evans encouraged bobbysoxers to form their own fan clubs, hold meetings and write letters to newspapers about their hero. Each fan club received a charter signed by Frank. Within months Evans was telling reporters there were more than 1,000 Sinatra fan clubs in the country. They had names like The Moonlit Sinatra Club, The Slaves of Sinatra, and The Flatbush Girls Who Would Lay Down Their Lives For Frank Sinatra Fan Club. At least 250 clubs published their own newspapers,[1] and Sinatra received an average 5,000 letters a week.[2] Social critics were appalled. They suggested most of his fans were overweight, plain girls from low-income families, who had few dates and little likelihood of ever having a boyfriend.[3] One Congressman named Frank as 'the prime instigator of juvenile delinquency in America'.

The hysteria around Sinatra was unprecedented. Teenage girls had swooned at Bing Crosby's gigs, but it was nothing compared with what happened at a Sinatra concert. Many asked what could be the cause of this mass delirium.

The US had entered the Second World War in 1942, turning the lives of millions of people upside down. Psychologists suggested the Sinatra phenomenon grew out of that experience. Absent fathers, husbands and boyfriends left a vacuum in people's lives. For many, music and cinema offered an escape from hardship and horror. The scarcity of eligible young men also made it 'safe' to project sexual fantasies on to an unobtainable object. Sinatra was unobtain-

able in two senses – he was a star and therefore out of reach, and he was 'happily married' to Nancy. The adoration of him touched on sexual emotions in the girls that many did not fully understand.

The singer himself said of his appeal to teenage girls: 'Psychologists have tried to go into the reasons why. Perfectly simple: it was the war years and there was a great loneliness. I was

Sinatra fans in a swoon

the boy in every drug store, the boy who'd gone off to war' .[4]

His popularity also coincided with the development of youth culture, making him the first teen idol – the original pop icon. In the past, childhood had been short. Before the First World War, many children began work at the age of 12 or 13. By the Second World War the school leaving age had risen to 15-16. In addition, more working class children were going on to college. These young people had more spending power than their predecessors, and they spent it on clothes, make-up and music.

The 1940s saw the first million-selling singles in the US.

Bing Crosby's 'White Christmas' (1942) sold about 30 million copies and Glenn Miller's 1942 recording of 'Chattanooga Choo Choo' was also a million-seller.[5] Yet not even Crosby had hit the million mark throughout the 1930s.[6] This process speeded up through the 1950s and 1960s. The value of record sales in the US rose from $10 million in 1931 to $260 million in 1956. By 1973 it had reached $2,000 million. Every member of the five to 19 age group in the US spent at least five times as much on records in 1970 as they had in 1955.[7] Frank was there at the start of this process, and he sailed right through it.

There was also another kind of female Sinatra fan – the Rosie the Riveter figure depicted in wartime factory recruitment posters. The Second World War opened up a number of jobs for women which had previously been the domain of men. These working class women could support themselves financially, and they asserted their right to be treated equally. They demanded 'liberation', even if it only involved the right to smoke, drink and sleep around like their male counterparts.

Top: women riveters working during the war years. Above: the front of a UAW booklet

Sinatra also had a big impact on young men. Many liked his singing and often aped his fashion style – wide-shouldered jackets and bowties. But others were not so keen. There is a famous photograph of a group of sailors pelting an advertisement for a Sinatra concert with tomatoes. The reason was simple: while millions of young American men went off to war

– and your average GI Joe earned $40 a month and probably wouldn't see his Mary Lou for several years – Sinatra stayed at home. He had been rejected for military service because, among other things, he had a perforated eardrum. To add insult to injury, Sinatra was earning $1 million a year and probably sweeping young Mary Lou off her feet.

Yet for millions, including many in the armed forces, Sinatra's voice expressed beautifully their feelings of love, loneliness and longing. The titles of the songs said it all – 'Saturday Night (Is The Loneliest Night Of The Week)', 'I'll Be Seeing You', 'When Your Lover Has Gone' and 'Homesick That's All'. One of the definitive Sinatra songs of the era was 'Nancy (With the Laughing Face)', released in 1945. The song, written by comedian Phil Silvers, was inspired by the singer's daughter, Nancy. Sinatra's song to his little girl made servicemen think about their own wives and daughters back home. As Gene Lees wrote in *Downbeat* magazine, 'He said for the boys what they wanted to say. He said to the girls what they wanted to hear'.[8]

Sinatra was, by now, the ultimate interpreter of American popular song, a form which had reached its peak by the 1940s. Songwriter George Gershwin was already dead, and Cole Porter and Irving Berlin had by then produced their best work. These and other songwriters, including Johnny Mercer and Rodgers and Hart, wrote songs for urban audiences who wanted to be entertained and escape the drudgery of everyday life. They made their livings writing scores for musicals and films, bringing together big band jazz, African-American rhythms, and European melodic structures and

Frank in the studio, Liederkrantz Hall, New York, 1947
Photo: William P Gottlieb

harmonies to create a vibrant and confident sound. Sinatra also played a major role in using the microphone to revolutionise stage performances. The microphone removed the requirement to sing in high registers in order to be heard above the band. He was one of the first popular performers to use the microphone as an instrument, using it to create a mood, and vocal variation and tone.

Despite his success, Sinatra stayed out of the recording studio for the first two years of his solo career. He had a recording contract with Columbia Records. But the year he left the Tommy Dorsey Band, the American Federation of Musicians union went on strike against the recording companies, demanding payments for songs performed on the radio. The strike was a long one. After a year, two young record labels, Capitol and Decca, negotiated a deal with the union. But Frank's label, Columbia, held out for a further year. Sinatra later talked of this period on a radio programme. 'I was a hold out,' he said. 'I really held out. I think the strike went on for a couple of years... I didn't want to cross the lines'.[9] However, he did record a number of a cappella songs during this time – they did not break the strike because they did not use musicians.

Three days after the strike ended, Sinatra and his producer Axel Stordahl went into the studio to make their first true recording of 'If You Are A Dream'. From then on the partnership between Sinatra and Stordahl kept the hits rolling in. Stordahl's sweet, jazz-tinged arrangements played a big part in creating the Sinatra sound. Frank's vocal sound had also changed – he had moved away from his crooning style towards something more expressive and poetic.

Sinatra's success had a profound impact on American music. He played a major role in making the vocalist the main attraction and pushing bands into the background. The Sinatra sound, coupled with the arrival of bebop – a new form of jazz – signalled the end of big band jazz.

There was one final, major change in music during this period – the explosion in sales of the 78rpm record. By 1946, Sinatra was selling 10 million records a year.[10] He was also branching out into radio and film. Sinatra signed to RKO pictures and made a series of films, including *Anchors Aweigh* (1945) and *It Happened in Brooklyn* (1946). Both are patriotic, feel-good musicals which fitted a country adjusting to life after the war.

Frank under pressure

Between 1942 and 1947 Sinatra reached the peak of the pop world with his interpretations of popular American songs. He was the country's biggest-selling artist. He earned $100,000 per film, $4,500 per concert and $1,000 for each personal appearance. He played the most prestigious venues in the US, and a kiss from Frank at a charity night would cost you $100!

It was in the midst of this success that Frank made a political decision. He would openly back Roosevelt's bid to extend his presidency and throw himself into the struggle against racism.

04 / The house I live in: Frank and the Popular Front

A new stage in Sinatra's life began with a simple letter to the president, Franklin D Roosevelt, in 1944. Throughout the remainder of the decade, Sinatra would frequently act as a champion of the poor and oppressed. The note he sent was short, but heartfelt:

My Dear Mr President
Are those guys kidding? We're winning the war.
Yours sincerely
Frank Sinatra

He wrote in response to the attacks on Roosevelt by the Republican Party and the press. A few days after sending the letter, Frank was invited for tea at the White House. On his way inside he told reporters, 'I want to talk to the president about his political campaign because I would like to do all I can to help'.[1] And help is what he did. He joined the Political Action Committee (PAC) which had been set up by the trade union federation, the Congress of Industrial Organisations (CIO). The secretary of the committee was Sidney Hillman,

who led the Amalgamated Clothing Workers of America (ACWA) and was one of the founders of the CIO. The PAC organised voter registration drives in the run-up to the election. Its slogan was 'Every worker a voter'.

Sinatra played his part in the 1944 election campaign. He donated $5,000 to the Democrats, the equivalent of $50,000 today. He encouraged his fans to wear badges bearing the slogan 'Frankie's for FDR and so are we', and he spoke at a huge Democratic Party rally at Madison Square Gardens. Sinatra told the rally the youth of America were entitled to the coming peace, but said, 'This peace will depend on your parents' votes.' He also made radio broadcasts in support of FDR. In the last few days of the campaign he appeared at two or three political events a day.[2] At the same time, Bing Crosby announced he was backing the Republican Party.

Frank talking to the youth of America

The night FDR won the election, Sinatra and the actor and director Orson Welles toured the bars of New York, ending their night at the headquarters of the clothing workers' union, which was in the same building as the Communist Party HQ.

Sinatra had privately supported the Democrats and FDR from an early age. But it was a brave move to go public. He was one of the first stars to declare his political affiliation. The right-wing press rounded on him, and he was warned by a reporter that it would hurt his career. Sinatra countered, 'Well, the hell with that. I'm more inter-

ested in good government than in my own future'.[3]

After the election, Sinatra's politics took a turn to the left. Roosevelt's victory appeared to embolden him. Sinatra addressed numerous left-wing rallies, actively supported the struggle against racism and for civil rights, and was an articulate opponent of fascism. To under-

With Eleanor Roosevelt and a statue of Franklin D

stand why a major star would make such a stand and jeopardise his career you have to look at the political radicalisation in America in the 1930s and early 1940s.

The 1930s was a decade of despair in many respects. Hitler and the Nazi Party came to power in Germany in 1933, Franco and his fascists were on the march in Spain, and mass unemployment stalked the world. But it was also a period of resistance. In Spain, the working class rose up to defend the Republic and kept Franco at bay for three years. There were mass strikes in France against the threat of fascism, and all over Europe the unemployed fought for the right to work.

American workers were not immune to this spirit of resistance. A powerful social movement was forged in the US around three key campaigns – anti-fascism, anti-lynching and the industrial trade unionism of the CIO. Rallies in support of the Spanish Republic drew thousands into the struggle against fascism. Twenty years before Martin Luther King's Civil Rights Movement, organisations such as the Communist Party and the National Association for the Advancement of Colored People (NAACP) began to challenge the racism of the American South, with its Jim Crow segregation and lynch mob terror.

This working class militancy went through a period of offensive struggles and retreats. But 1934 was the defining year. Mass strikes led by socialists, Trotskyists and Communist Party members in the cities of Toledo, Minneapolis and San Francisco took on and defeated the bosses. Yet the radicalisation did not stop there. Hundreds of thousands of workers in the new mass production industries, who had previously been ignored by the craft unions of the American Federation of Labor (AFL), began to get organised. John L Lewis of the mineworkers' union and Sidney Hillman of the Amalgamated Clothing Workers Union, along with smaller industrial unions, broke from the AFL and set up a new federation, the Congress for Industrial Organisations (CIO). The CIO did not organise along craft lines, it organised all the workers in a single plant. And a new form of strike developed, called the sit-down strike. Instead of walking out of a factory and setting up picket lines, workers occupied their workplaces. In 1936 there were 48 sit-down strikes. In 1937 there were 477.[4]

The final defeat of the Spanish Republic, the Nazi-Soviet Pact and the onset of World War Two made 1939 a crisis point for the left. But it was also a year which saw one of the largest strike waves in US history. At the same time, Philip Randolph was leading the movement for a March on Washington which would win black workers jobs in the armaments industries. The first black member of a city council, Adam Clayton Powell, was elected in New York, as was the first Communist Party city councillor, Pete Cacchione.

There was another upswing in resistance in late 1945 and early 1946, when the CIO launched a huge strike wave – over one quarter of its membership went on strike, and there were general strikes in six major cities.

The Communist Party played a central role in this period of militancy, despite being a relatively small organisation. It claimed a membership of 75,000 in 1938, but half lived in the New York area.[5] It was also full of contradictions. On the one hand, its members included some of the most influential union militants and anti-racist campaigners in America. On the other hand, it supported the policies of Stalin and every twist and turn of Russian foreign policy, which in turn shaped the politics and direction of the party.

From 1928 to 1935 the Communist Party argued that social democrats – such as the British Labour Party and Germany's SPD – were as big a threat to the struggle for socialism as the fascists. Moscow laid down this line, which is known today as Third Period Stalinism. It was a policy which cut off the Communist Party militants from huge numbers of workers and intellectuals. Then in July 1935 the party made a U-turn. Delegates from 65 Communist parties met in Moscow and adopted a new line pushed by Stalin, who had woken up to the threat Hitler posed to Russia and wanted to make alliances with France and Britain. Communists were now expected to distinguish between bourgeois democracies, such as the US, and reactionary dictatorships.[6] They were to seek pacts with so-called progressive sections of the ruling class in their own countries. Such alliances were known as Popular Fronts or People's Fronts. As a consequence, between 1936 and 1938 the US Communist Party switched to supporting FDR.

The Popular Front in America gained enormous support and prestige during the Second World War as the Soviet Union and the US collaborated to defeat Hitler. The Communist Party argued that if people stood together, regardless of party or class, the threat of fascism could be defeated. The feeling of the time was summed up by US vice-president Henry Wallace in a speech in 1942, when he claimed the world was entering 'the Century of the Common Man'.

But there were at least three major political problems with the Popular Front strategy. First, although the left and sections of the ruling class agreed on stopping Hitler, they disagreed on most other issues. The effect of the Popular Front was to blunt criticism of FDR's anti working class policies at home and abroad.[7] Second, the Popular Front strategy of preserving unity with the government led the Communist Party to hold back struggles by workers. Third, sections of the ruling class were prepared to endorse the Popular Front strategy as long as it suited them. But they would drop the left as soon as the war was over, leaving many militants confused and disorientated.

Nonetheless, this flowering of radical protest had a massive impact on culture. The two became entwined. There was an explosion of artistic movements in the US like nothing seen before or since. The poet Langston Hughes, writers Richard Wright and John Dos Passos, musicians Duke Ellington, Billie Holiday and Woody Guthrie, singer and actor Paul Robeson, Orson Welles and a large number of less well known artists, painters, writers and poets used their talents to support the radical causes of the day. This revival of the arts was helped by the fact that the government gave money to artistic projects as part of its New Deal. Thousands of unemployed actors, writers and musicians worked for the Federal Arts Project. Plays were put on for working class audiences, murals painted on public buildings, and hundreds of pamphlets published.

This movement went through two key phases. During the 1930s the art was centred on the representation of working class life and struggles, in works such as Marc Blitzstein's play *The Cradle Will Rock* (1937) and the musical of the garment workers' union, *Pins and Needles* (1937). These themes were also expressed in the John Dos Passos novel *USA* (1930-36) and John Steinbeck's bestseller *The Grapes of Wrath* (1939). Woody Guthrie's *Dust Bowl Ballads* (1940) is another good example.

In contrast, much of the later art was heavily influenced by the politics of the Popular Front. Examples include composer Aaron Copeland's 'Fanfare For The Common Man'

(1942), Paul Robeson's 'Ballad For Americans' (1939), and Frank Capra's films *Mr Smith Goes To Washington* (1939) and *It's A Wonderful Life* (1946).

At the same time, as culture became increasingly industrialised through the 20th century it became a battleground between those who created art and those who owned and sold it. During the 1930s and 1940s there were a number of important campaigns for union recognition by screenwriters, film studio workers, cartoonists and musicians. There were also struggles to end discrimination and racist practices in cultural industries. Hollywood employed very few black actors, most orchestras did not hire black musicians, and concert halls and nightclubs refused to allow black musicians to play. Even some unions were separated along racial lines.

This blooming of radical culture in the US in the period has been called the Cultural Front. As historian Michael Denning writes, 'The Cultural Front was a common metaphor of the time, combining two meanings of the word "front": the military metaphor designating a place, a site of struggle or battlefront; and the political metaphor designating a group, a coalition with a common purpose'.[8] In part it was a result of the encounter between a powerful democratic social movement and the development of mass entertainment. Some of the artists involved in the Cultural Front were members of the Communist Party, others were fellow travellers, but many were simply liberals who were inspired by the exciting events.

Sinatra was a child of this movement. Many of those

involved in the Cultural Front influenced his artistic and political ideas. Sinatra may have arrived late on the scene, but his political and musical contributions helped shape this movement. At first, his proclamations were effective but naive. Even before the US entered the Second World War, Frank had wanted to take on the country's Nazis. An article in *Look Magazine* published soon after the war recorded an earlier Sinatra idea:

'Sinatra is still under 30, and obviously has many vigorous years ahead of him. So he seems likely to give further evidence of his belief in direct action as a means of indicating his approval or disapproval of other men's beliefs. Here is one plan with which his fancy has already toyed; he hasn't had an opportunity yet to put it into effect:

'It concerns an idea for interrupting, if not disrupting, political rallies being held by American pro-fascists. As everyone knows, these are people among whom Sinatra is cordially disliked because of the liberal slant of his views on public affairs. Sinatra's plan is simple and potentially quite effective. He proposes to attend such right-wing gatherings in person, accompanied by a retinue of 50 picked bobbysoxers of demonstrated lung power. They are to take seats up front, close to the speaker's platform. Then, whenever a speaker begins to utter some thought that Sinatra deems unfit for public consumption, the singer plans to touch his right cheek with his right forefinger. At this previously arranged cue, his chorus of 50 would burst into so clamorous a shriek that no other sound would come near reaching the audience's ears.

'"They'd never hear the guy trying to speak," Sinatra once said, as he described the scene in anticipation. He ought to know, many of his fellow citizens have been prevented by just some shrill outburst from hearing him when he has tried to sing.

'Sinatra has been much criticised for his willingness to express his political beliefs publicly. But along with a great many other patriotic entertainers, he sees no reason why his professional calling should limit his rights of citizenship. He is partial to speaking up. And he justifies his doing so by saying, "Even a crooner can yell when he wants to"'.[9]

Sinatra immersed himself in struggles and radical ideas. As soon as the 1944 election was over, he was telling journalists that he was avidly reading progressive books. He told one reporter, 'I started with the most prolific books – I mean the kind that are easily understandable to a person like me, with a newly found job in my mind and in my heart.' He said he had read *The History of Bigotry in the United States* by Gustavus Myers, *The American Dilemma* by Gunnar Myrdal, a study of blacks in the US, and *Freedom Road* by Howard Fast.[10] The blacklisted actor Lionel Stander said of Sinatra, 'He was one of the few actors who was able and willing to read Marx'.[11]

Frank also supported a large number of radical organisations associated with the Popular Front. He was vice-president of the Independent Citizens Committee of the Arts, Sciences and Professions in 1946, and a member of both American Youth for Democracy and the Progressive Citizens of America. He joined the short-lived Committee for the First Amendment (CFA), which sought to organise public support for the screenwriters and directors called before the House Un-American Activities Committee (HUAC). And he supported – and in some cases sponsored – the Joint Anti-Fascist Refugee Committee, the American Crusade to End Lynching, and Popular Front publications such as *The New Masses* and *PM*. The House Un-American Activities Committee would later deem many of these organisations to be Communist fronts.

In 1945, Sinatra intervened in a series of racist strikes at schools where parents and teachers opposed integration. He also went to a high school in the Bronx to talk to students about juvenile delinquency, under the watchful eye of his liberal publicity agent George Evans.[12] But it was the anti-racist cause that truly ignited Sinatra's passion, and he vowed to take his campaign to his young fans. He argued, 'I'll never forget how it hurt when kids called me a "Dago" when I was a boy. It's a scar that lasted a long time and which I have never quite forgotten. It isn't the kids' fault – it's their parents. They would never learn to make racial and religious discriminations if they didn't hear that junk at home'.[13]

Sinatra attempted to break down racial barriers, both in his personal life and his career. Orson Welles later told Nancy Sinatra of one encounter Frank had with a racist: 'We drove to his uncle's house for calamari and on the way back we stopped for coffee. Our driver as it happened was a black man, and the guy in the diner wouldn't serve him. Your dad reached across the counter and grabbed this nine-foot giant by the front of his shirt and said, "You're serving coffee for three." After a beat the man said, "Yes". No sporting event here. It was a mosquito vs a gorilla. Frank made the score with just sheer force of character'.[14]

He also fought to end discrimination in the film and recording industry. Musician Milt Bernhart recalled, 'When Frank had a record date he bent over backwards to try and find black musicians who could play the music.' Guitarist Al Viola remembered that Sinatra 'always insisted on having integrated orchestras'. Even the musicians' union was segregated in Hollywood. Sinatra ended that when he hired black flautist Buddy Collette to play in his band.[15]

Even something as minor as a photograph could challenge racist stereotypes. In 1943 Sinatra and black singer Hazel Scott posed for a picture. The idea of a black woman and white man sitting together in a photograph was regarded as risque at the time. But what shocked the bigots was the fact that they were holding hands. For good measure, Scott was an active member of the burgeoning civil rights movement and an open supporter of the Communist Party.

When it came to the struggle for civil rights, Frank said, 'I'm in it for life.' Yet it was the short film *The House I Live In* and the song of the same title that really put Sinatra's commitment to the anti-racist cause on the map. The ten-minute film by RKO was a classic of the Popular Front era. It shows a group of schoolchildren abusing a young Jewish boy. Sinatra emerges from the studio, calls the boys over and says:

'Look, fellas, religion doesn't make any difference except to a Nazi or a dope. Don't let them make a sucker out of you. God didn't create one people better than another. Your blood is the same as mine, and mine is the same as his. You know what this country is? It's made up of a hundred different kinds of people – and they're all Americans…Let's use our good American brains and not fight each other.' Then Sinatra sings:

What is America to me?
A name a map, or a flag I see,
A certain word, democracy
What is America to me?

The house I live in
A plot of earth, a street
The grocer and the butcher
Or the people that I meet.

The children in the playground,
The faces that I see
All races and religions
That's America to me.

The place I work in
The worker by my side
The little town, the city
Where my people lived and died

The howdy and the handshake
The air a feeling free
And the right to speak your mind out
That's America to me

The things I see about me
The big things and the small
That little corner newsstand
Or the house a mile tall

The wedding and the churchyard
The laughter and the tears
And the dream that's been a growing
For more than two hundred years

The town I live in
The street, the house, the room
The pavement of the city
Or the garden all in bloom

The church, the school, the clubhouse
The million lights I see
But especially the people – yes, especially the people
That's America to me

The film was directed by Mervyn LeRoy and shot in two days in May 1945, shortly after the sudden death of President Roosevelt. Both Sinatra and LeRoy received Oscars for the film the following year.

Abel Meeropol wrote the lyrics of the song under the pen name Lewis Allan. Meeropol, a schoolteacher from New York, is more famous as the man who wrote 'Strange Fruit', the song immortalised by Billie Holiday. Meeropol and his wife would adopt the orphaned sons of Ethel and Julius Rosenberg – two Communists executed during the coming McCarthyite era after being accused of spying.[16]

The music was written by Earl Robinson, who also composed 'Ballad For Americans' and 'Joe Hill', two classic songs from the Popular Front era. Both were made famous by Paul Robeson. Sinatra also recorded a version of 'Ballad For Americans'. The film's scriptwriter was Albert Maltz, another important cultural figure in the Communist Party, who would later become famous as one of the Hollywood Ten.

The studio insisted on cutting several lines from 'The House I Live In'. In the second verse, the line 'My neighbors white and black' was removed, as was the line, 'The worker and the farmer'. The cuts enraged Meeropol.[17] But it showed the power of corporations to control and dictate how art is presented and disseminated. It also demonstrated the weakness of the Popular Front political message in classic songs of the period, such as 'The House I Live In', 'Ballad For Americans' and Woody Guthrie's 'This Land Is Your Land'. The populist and nationalist sentiments expressed in such songs made it easy to distort the message and subvert them into right-wing anthems. Sinatra would later do this himself with his 1970s rendition of 'The House I Live In'.

Scenes from the short film The House I Live In

The money Sinatra made from *The House I Live In* was donated to the California Labor School, founded in 1942. The school had four departments – one each for union organising, creative writing, social sciences and industrial arts. The teachers were mainly union officials and local college teachers. Orson Welles, poet Muriel Rukeyser and architect Frank Lloyd Wright all spoke at the school.[18]

Frank's commitment to fighting racism led him to visit Benjamin Franklin High School in Italian Harlem, New York, in October 1945. It was the scene of fighting between Italian-American and black students. The great jazz saxophone player Sonny Rollins was a student at the school at the time. He recalled, 'Sinatra came down there and sang in our auditorium…after that, things got better and the rioting stopped'.[19] According to eyewitnesses, Sinatra sang 'Aren't You Glad You're You' and 'The House I Live In'.[20] A contingent of 600 students carried placards declaring 'Americans All – Negro, Jewish, Catholic and Protestant'.[21]

The success of *The House I Live In* also led Sinatra to Froebel High School in Gary, Indiana. This was the scene of a strike by white students against a new principal who was trying to introduce anti-racist policies. He allowed the school's 270 black students to share classrooms with whites, to join the school orchestra and to swim in the school pool one day a week. More than 1,000 white students walked out and refused to return as long as they had to share facilities with the black students. Their parents supported them, fearing competition for their jobs in the steel mills from Gary's growing black population.

After four days, Sinatra turned up in Gary on 1 November 1945. George Evans and Jack Keller escorted him into the school auditorium, where more than 5,000 pupils and parents had gathered. Jack Keller recalled:

'Frank walked out onstage and stood dead centre while all these rough, tough steel workers and their kids started cat-calling and whistling and stamping their feet. Frank folded his arms, looked right down at them and stared for a full two minutes, until there was a dead silence in the room. Evans and I were nervous wrecks wondering what the hell he was going to do.

'Without smiling, Frank kept staring at the audience. Finally he unfolded his arms and moved to the microphone and said, "I can lick any son of a bitch in this joint." Pandemonium broke out as the kids cheered him. They thought he was right down their street and from then on it was terrific.

'Frank spoke earnestly: "I implore you to return to school. This is a bad deal kids. It's not good for you and it's not good for the city of Gary, which has done so much to help with the war for freedom the world over. Believe me, I know something about the business of racial intolerance. At 11 I was called a 'dirty Guinea' back home in New Jersey." "No, no, no" shrieked hundreds of girls in the audience. "No, Frankie, no." "We've all done it," he said. "We've all used the words nigger or kike or Mick or Polack or Dago. Cut it out kids. Go back to school. You've got to go back because you don't want to be ashamed of your student body, your city, your country."

'He pointed out that the Nazis used the method of divide and rule by pitting race against race. "Don't let it happen here," he pleaded. "I learned that a few people who have nothing to do with the Gary schools, who aren't even parents, have interfered and helped foment this trouble. Don't listen to them. Sit down and talk it over. If President Roosevelt could do it with Churchill and Stalin, then the kids of America can work out their problems too."

'Frank finished by singing two songs and asking the kids to rise and repeat with him a pledge for tolerance: "We will strive to work together to prove that the American way is the only fair and democratic way of life." Then everyone sang the national anthem'.[22]

Frank didn't end the strike at Froebel High School, but no other major recording star of the period laid his reputation on the line in such a fashion. In 1947 Sinatra made the following statement against racism:

'We've got a hell of a way to go in this racial situation. As long as most white men think of a Negro as a Negro first and a man second, we're in trouble. I don't know why we can't grow up. It took us long enough to get past the stage where we were calling all Italians "Wops" and "Dagos", but if we don't drop this "nigger" thing, we just won't be around much longer. Hell, actors have got to take a stand politically, even if we're afraid we'll get hurt at the box office'.[23]

As well as 'The House I Live In', Sinatra recorded two other songs which implicitly reinforced his anti-racist message. The first was 'Ol' Man River', which he recorded in 1943-44. The great black artist Paul Robeson had first sung this song from the musical *Show Boat* in 1927. Robeson had turned the show tune into a dignified lament about an unequal world. But Robeson had no choice other than to stick to the original lyrics which included the line 'Darkies all worked on the Mississippi'. Twenty years later Sinatra's version was just as powerful. However, Frank was able to change the lyrics to, 'Here we all work while the white folks play'.

Vibraphonist Emile Richardson explained why the song not only packed a powerful political punch but also worked as a magnificent musical statement: 'He [Sinatra] would hold his hands behind his back as if he were handcuffed, pull his shoulders forward, or his chest forward and his shoulders back, to get more air. He would go "Tote that barge / Lift that bale / Get a little drunk and you land in jailll"... and without a pause for breath would go right into "I get weary".'[24]

Sinatra's vocal range during this period was breathtaking. It extended all the way up to the falsetto note he used to climax on the Alex Stordahl arrangement of 'This Song Is You' – a very high F (two Fs above middle C) and right down to the low G on 'Ol' Man River'.

The second song he recorded was 'Lost in the Stars' (1946). This was written by the former Communist Kurt Weill. It is an abstract song, but deals with the deep alienation that racism creates. Sinatra would return to 'Ol'Man River' and 'Lost In The Stars' when he came out in support of Martin Luther King's Civil Rights Movement in the 1960s.

Many writers claim that Sinatra was nothing more than a good, old-fashioned liberal. But I believe his ideas and actions went further than this. With the exception of Paul Robeson, no other mainstream artist made such a stand. Sinatra went far beyond the kind of politics espoused by FDR and the New Deal Democrats. He was prepared to work with the Communist left and use his talents to challenge the system, and he made a unique contribution to the struggle against racism. This did not go unnoticed by the right-wing press or the vultures in the Republican Party. With the Second World War over, they aimed to break the left, and Sinatra was firmly in their sights.

05 / When no one cares: the bad years

'Are you now or have you ever been a member of the Communist Party?' That question was to haunt US society for more than a generation. From 1947 until the end of the 1950s, a series of Congressional hearings in Washington, New York and Los Angeles led to a witch-hunt of epic proportions.

More than 20,000 workers lost their jobs, and dozens of Communist Party members were imprisoned. Screen idol Charlie Chaplin was banned from entering the country, and Paul Robeson was prevented from leaving it. In a grisly climax, Ethel and Julius Rosenberg were executed for allegedly passing atomic secrets to the Russians. The witch-hunt and the blacklist cast a dark shadow over US society, with the House Un-American Activities Committee (HUAC) at its heart.

To make sense of the fear that gripped the country you have to understand the changes the US underwent after the Second World War. In 1946, America's rulers were rocked by an upswing of working class revolt led by the CIO. But it was the growing tension with Russia that shaped the next decade. By 1948 the world was divided into two camps – one under the control of Stalin's Soviet Union and the other under the influence of the US and its Western allies. Military expenditure hit unprecedented levels, rising to 20 percent of US national output and up to 40 percent of Russia's as Stalin tried to keep up.[1] The two superpowers organised rival military alliances – Nato and the Warsaw Pact. Although the US was militarily stronger than Russia and its allies, both sides had nuclear weapons. Tensions were high as the Cold War began. Berlin was blockaded and China came under the control of Mao and his Communist Party. Then the US became embroiled in the Korean War.

The American establishment pumped out anti-Communist propaganda which permeated deep into society. The Taft-Hartley law required trade unions to purge Communist officials from their ranks and banned secondary strike action. Schoolchildren all over the country participated in mock air raids and nuclear attacks, as comic strip hero Captain America warned, 'Beware Commies, spies, traitors and foreign agents! Captain America, with all loyal, free men behind him, is looking for you'.[2] The atmosphere created by the Cold War made it easier to win over a section of the population to support rearmament, and helped curb working class militancy.

The witch-hunt began at the top with Democratic president Harry Truman, who sacked government workers who belonged to the Communist Party. A number of leading Democrats who had supported or at least tolerated the Popular Front now turned on the left. The director of the FBI, J Edgar Hoover, handed the names of Communists and former Communists to the HUAC. However, it was Republican Senator Joe McCarthy whose name became synonymous with the witch-hunts. McCarthy and his right-wing zealots waged an unrelenting war on what he described as 'Communist infiltration' of Hollywood and the entertainment industry. Two of McCarthy's leading supporters in Hollywood were Walt Disney and Ronald Reagan.

In 1947, the HUAC descended on Hollywood and the show trials began. Nineteen Hollywood screenwriters and directors were summoned to Washington to answer the question, 'Are you now or have you ever been…' It signalled the end of the Cultural Front – the alliance of Communists, fellow travelers and progressives shattered, although many artists fought a rearguard action.

Sinatra came out publicly in support of the Hollywood 19. He joined a long list of stars, including Humphrey Bogart, John Huston, Gene Kelly, Katherine Hepburn, Burt Lancaster, Ava Gardner and Henry Fonda, in making a stand against the HUAC. They set up an organisation called the Committee for the First Amendment, which was branded a Communist front by the FBI. Sinatra added his signature to a petition by more than 300 Hollywood luminaries which argued:

'We the undersigned, as American Citizens who believe in constitutional democratic government, are disgusted and outraged by the continuing attempt by the House Committee on Un-American Activities to smear the Motion Picture Industry.

'We hold that these hearings are morally wrong because: any investigation into the political beliefs of the individual is contrary to the basic principles of our democracy.

'Any attempt to curb freedom of expression and to set arbitrary standards of Americanism is in itself disloyal to both the spirit and letter of the Constitution'.[3]

On 25 October 1947, Sinatra joined a group of Hollywood celebrities – including Humphrey Bogart, Lauren Bacall, Rita Hayworth, Groucho Marx and Gene Kelly – at a meeting at Ira Gershwin's home to organise a higher-profile campaign. Gershwin would later give the California Un-American Activities Committee the names of those who had attended the meeting at his home.[4]

Sinatra, Judy Garland and a host of other celebrities took part in a coast to coast radio broadcast entitled 'Hollywood Fights Back'. The great band leader Artie Shaw ended the show by saying, 'The HUAC wants to approve the notes we play and the words we say…When freedom goes, most of the good things in American life go with it. Better get off the bandstand Mr Thomas, nobody's dancing!' Thomas was the right-wing zealot who chaired the hearing.[5]

Sinatra flew into Washington to join Bogart, Bacall, Gene Kelly and Groucho Marx in supporting those called before the committee.[6] He made one of the most brave and powerful condemnations of the HUAC:

'Once they get the movies throttled, how long will it be before the committee goes to work on freedom of the air? How long will it be before we're told what we can say and what we cannot say into a radio microphone? If you can make a pitch on a nationwide radio network for a square deal for the underdog, will they call you a Commie? Are they going to scare us into silence, I wonder?'[7]

The hearing was nothing short of scandalous. It was a show trial with the world's media in attendance. Eleven of the 19 were called to testify. Ten refused to comment on *The HUAC in* their political beliefs, citing the First Amendment of the US *full swing* Constitution. The German playwright Bertolt Brecht was the eleventh to testify. He confused his interrogators with his answers and then left the country. With eight more witnesses to call, the committee just shut up shop. The ten who had cited the First Amendment were charged with contempt, convicted and jailed. They were Alvah Bessie, Herbert Biberman, Lester Cole, Edward Dmytryk, John Howard Lawson, Ring Lardner Jr, Albert Maltz, Samuel Ornitz, Adrian Scott and Dalton Trumbo. Together, they became known as the Hollywood Ten.

The protest by the stars in Washington was brave and clearly boosted the morale of those facing the witch-hunt, but it was not enough to stop the McCarthyite juggernaut cutting a swathe through Hollywood.

Lauren Bacall told the *Washington Daily News*, 'I attended two sessions of the hearings and it frightened me. I don't want to alarm you, but I think you should be aware of the dangers. When they start telling you what pictures you can make, what your subjects can be, then it's time to rear up and fight! It starts with us but I'm sorry to say it won't end with us.' Bacall was right. The government was using the show trials to tell ordinary people, 'If we can break the people in Hollywood, just think what we can do to you'.[8]

The main target of the HUAC was not Hollywood at all. The attacks on the artists and screenwriters were a way of getting at the real enemy – organised labour and working class militants. Official figures show more than 20,000 trade unionists lost their jobs as a result of the McCarthyite witch-hunts. But many more trade union activists were driven out of their places of work.

Sinatra described the years between 1947 and 1953 as his 'Dark Ages'. His career took a nosedive. He had recorded 15 hit singles in 1946. But between 1947 and 1953 nothing he released was a hit.[9] In 1950, the movie mogul Louis B Mayer cancelled Sinatra's film contract with MGM, and in 1952 Columbia Records officially ended his recording contract.

There were a number of reasons for Sinatra's fall from grace – his connections with the Mafia, a high-octane affair with actress Ava Gardner, and his poor choice of recording material. But the attempts by the press and the FBI to label him a Communist were also damaging.

Jack Tenney, chairman of the California State Senate Committee on Un-American Investigations, accused Sinatra of being a Communist. So did the notorious racist leader of the America First party, Gerald L K Smith. Sinatra rebuffed the accusations, telling the *Daily Worker*, 'Somebody said I spoke like a Communist. You know, they call Shirley Temple a Communist too. Well, I said, me and Shirley both, I guess'.[10]

Hundreds of pamphlets denouncing 'Commies' were produced in the late 1940s and 1950s. The 1948 pamphlet *Red Betrayal Of Youth*, by Kenneth Goff, gives a flavour:

'Of late this young Red punk [Sinatra] has been touring the country swooning bobbysoxers with his baritone voice while he tells their parents how to vote. He appeared before 16,000 left-wingers in Madison Square Gardens last year at the opening of a nationwide campaign by the Communist Party and the New Deal's "Russian Firsters" to capture the veterans' votes.

'Frank Sinatra, defiant in bow tie, demanded freedom for the Chinese; a campaign against the Spanish Government; and public recognition of the political possibilities of radio crooners. While Sinatra and others demanded the over-throwing of Franco, Red Fascists passed out handbills in the crowd, which read, "Veterans–Join the Communist Party... Our party stands for the ownership and control of the nation's economy by the workers and farmers."

'Through this one performance alone any intelligent person ought to be able to see how "Red Frankie" with his gentle purring voice is swooning the youth of America into the arms of atheistic Communism'.[11]

Today this kind of stuff seems comical. But at the time, pamphlets like this could destroy someone's life. The HUAC used them as evidence. Between 1945 and 1953 Sinatra was named as a Communist in front of the HUAC 12 times.[12] The FBI would keep him under surveillance for almost 40 years, compiling a 1,275-page dossier on him. The largest part of the FBI file is comprised of reports linking him to the 'Mob', but almost 25 percent is devoted to Sinatra's involvement with the left.

The FBI conducted a thorough investigation of Sinatra's links with the Communist Party. Although a couple of informants claimed Sinatra was actually a member, most just linked him to Communist fronts.

But I think Jo-Caroll Silvers, wife of comedian Phil Silvers, had the true measure of the man. She remembered, 'Frank was such an ardent liberal in those days. So concerned about poor people that he was always quoting Henry Wallace. We both shared this political bond, more so than anyone else in our social group. In fact, both Frank and I were fairly close to the Communist Party line at that time. Neither of us were card-carrying members of course, but we were both very close to people like Albert Maltz who were, and we shared their beliefs for the most part'.[13]

What is undeniable is that Sinatra worked closely with the Communist Party. Many of his friends and associates were members or fellow travellers of the party. In fact, even his dentist was a member of the party! [14]

Sinatra's support for Progressive Party candidate Henry

Wallace in 1947 increased the suspicions of the FBI. The Progressive Party was a left-led coalition which stood against President Truman of the Democratic Party. The Cold War had shattered the unity of the Popular Front. The Democratic Party moved to the right, and a number of liberals formed an organisation called Americans for Democratic Action. Its manifesto stated, 'We reject any association with Communism or sympathisers with Communism in the US as completely as we reject any association with Fascists or their sympathisers.' In effect, these Cold War liberals supported the witch-hunts.[15]

Partly as a reply to this, Sinatra wrote a letter to the *New Republic* magazine edited by Wallace. 'Prices are high and people are kicking about them and fear seems to have more to do with the insecurity of everybody's future,' he wrote. The letter argued for 'tolerance' among people of different backgrounds, adding, 'It was pretty easy to march with the liberals in the years of Roosevelt.' Sinatra wanted Wallace to offer the type of leadership which could re-establish unity between liberals and progressives.[16]

But the Wallace campaign ended in failure and the Communist Party was crushed out of existence, leaving Sinatra isolated. Many in the recording and film industries became nervous about his associations with the left. Over the next few years, Sinatra withdrew from supporting radical movements. By 1951, he was was prepared to take part in a rally in Central Park sponsored by the Stop Communism Committee.[17] Yet neither the FBI nor the federal government was satisfied with his public denunciations of

Communism. The US army even denied Sinatra clearance to entertain troops in Korea at Christmas.

It's important to remember that Sinatra never named names and, years later, he was remembered by many on the blacklist as a trusted and generous friend during the dark days of McCarthyism. Ring Lardner Jr, one of the Hollywood Ten, recalled Sinatra as among a small group of 'liberals...who continued a staunch defence of our rights'.[18] The actress Betsy Blair Reisz said Sinatra was always willing to give money to blacklisted actors in trouble: 'He didn't care to know and he didn't want to talk about it – but he did give.'

Other factors contributed to Sinatra's downward spiral. His choice of recording material was poor, although that had much to do with the period. McCarthyism had the effect of dumbing down culture. Everything became safe – feelgood films and musicals and novelty records were the order of the day. Sinatra released a number of novelty records himself. The low point was the embarrassing single 'Mama Will Bark', a duet with a B-list comedienne and singer named Dagmar. Sinatra crooned while a dog impersonator barked in the background. The song was a howler in every sense! Of course, there were still a few gems in Sinatra's discography – 'Hello Young Lovers' and the majestical 'I'm a Fool to Want You' are two obvious examples.

Sinatra recognised the problems with some of his material in a *Metronome* interview. He complained that most songwriters had to 'prostitute' their talents if they wanted 'to make a buck', because 'not enough publishers are buying the better kind of music'. Quality songs were available, but producers and record executives would 'rather take an easy song, one that is a novelty. It's a short shot that will click right away, but that doesn't last over the years. Most publishers don't think that far ahead'.[19]

Another factor in the collapse of Sinatra's career was his affair with Ava Gardner. Since the bobbysox years publicity agents had portrayed Sinatra as a happily married man. The image sold records. So when Sinatra was seen flaunting his affair with Gardner the press went into a frenzy. The pair were called 'home wreckers'. This kind of scandal could destroy a career in the 1940s and 1950s. When movie star Ingrid Bergman had a child outside marriage her films were pulled from cinemas. Similarly, when Sinatra left his wife, priests told kids not to buy his records.

Frank with Ava Gardner

Sinatra divorced Nancy and married Ava Gardner in 1951. Just like the affair, the marriage was shortlived and explosive. The destructive nature of the relationship helped Sinatra create one of his greatest songs, 'I'm A Fool To Want You'. It's an aching lament, sung by a man trying to come to terms with the guilt and loneliness of a love affair that is sinking into the abyss.

The final straw for Sinatra's career was his connection with the Mafia, and a string of confrontations – physical and verbal – with journalists. The most infamous of these saw Frank knock out right-wing columnist Lee Mortimer in April 1947.

By 1952, Sinatra's television work had dried up, his film career was in the doldrums and he was struggling to get a recording contract. He was labelled a friend of the Mafia, a thug and a Red. It would be a gross understatement to say things were not looking good. Yet in a few years Frank Sinatra would be back. A blockbuster film and a series of albums would confirm his status as one of the greatest singers of the century. Was this due to a horse's head in a bed? Or did it have more to do with Sinatra's talent?

Francis Ford Coppola's film masterpiece *The Godfather* begins with the wonderful scene of the wedding of the daughter of Mafia boss Don Corleone. Suddenly, hundreds of young girls start screaming as singing legend Johnny Fontaine arrives to perform. Coppola insists Johnny Fontaine is a fictional character, but sometimes truth can be stranger than fiction. In 1948 Sinatra sang at the wedding of mobster Willie Moretti's daughter.[1]

Sinatra was dogged by accusations that he was in the service of the Mafia throughout his career. It was something he always strenuously denied. He complained the charges were made because his 'surname ended in a vowel' – a reference to his Italian background. But testimony from Frank's friends and enemies, as well as FBI documents, suggest Sinatra's career was very much intertwined with the mob.

The Mafia's roots lie in Sicily.[2] According to folklore, the Mafia started out 600 years ago as an underground patriotic society which fought Arab, Norman, French and Spanish invaders. Like so many stories that glamorise the Mafia, it is untrue. The first mention of the Mafia in Sicily occurs around 1860. The Mafia emerged on two areas of the island – its members acted as debt collectors for absent landlords in western Sicily and around the prosperous lemon and orange farms near Palermo. Peasants, farmers and businessmen were all forced to pay protection money. Those who did not were brutally dealt with. The Mafia also rigged elections and bought off sections of the establishment.[3]

The Mafia in the US was the creation of a distinctly American experience. Immigrants to the country were politically, economically and culturally displaced. The state failed to provide adequate facilities for immigrant families and the police left the ghettoes to the mercy of gangs and racketeers. At best the establishment ignored what was going on, and in many instances there was collusion with the gangs. It was in this environment that the Mafia established itself in Italian communities. It could protect areas, arrange loans and settle disputes, but this came at a price. All immigrant communities had their own gangs – it wasn't an Italian thing. And the local gangster was strictly a local phenomenon, someone whose power only extended a few streets or blocks.

It was the introduction of Prohibition in 1920 that gave

rise to the modern Mafia. Bootlegging – the illegal production, distribution and sale of alcohol – became a multi-million dollar business. On the eve of Prohibition there were 15,000 licensed bars in New York. Within a few years there would be 32,000 illegal speakeasies selling alcohol in the city. This gave the smalltime gangsters an opportunity to expand their business. By the late 1920s and early 1930s a new generation of mobsters controlled the supply and distribution of alcohol. Contrary to popular belief, the Mafia did not restrict its membership to Sicilian immigrants. It became an alliance of Italian, Jewish and Irish mobsters – men like Longie Zwillman, Meyer Lansky, Lucky Luciano, Ben (Bugsy) Siegal and Frank Costello. It was a product of the Americanisation of crime.

The Mafia ran businesses like any venture capitalist would. There were takeovers, buyouts and liquidation sales. The difference was that lead was the currency of exchange. When Sinatra was growing up there were a number of violent turf wars. The most famous led to the St Valentine's Day Massacre in Chicago in 1929.[4] Authorised by Al Capone, this wiped out almost all his competition in one swoop.[5] In 1930-31 New York became a battleground as various Mafia groups fought for control of the city. Their battles were known as the Castellamarese Wars.

With the end of Prohibition in 1933, the Mafia diversified its business interests into drugs, gambling, prostitution and even trade unions. On occasions, its interests coincided with those of the American government. So in 1943 the Mafia helped the US military with its invasion of Sicily, and in the early 1960s the CIA and the Mafia colluded to try to get rid of Fidel Castro.

Far from being opposed to the state, the Mafia liked to work with the authorities. The wealthiest and most powerful Mafia bosses were those who had bought off judges, police departments and prohibition agents. This cost a lot of money, but it was better than facing a crackdown. In most cases, murder was a last resort – it was bad for business.

Sinatra once said of this period, 'Prohibition was the dumbest law in American history. It was never going to work, not ever. But what it did create was the mob. These dummies with their books and investigations, they think the mob was invented by a bunch of Sicilians in some smoky place. Probably in Palermo. Bullshit. The mob was invented by all those self-righteous bastards who gave us Prohibition. It was invented by ministers, Southern politicians, by all the goddamned idiots who think they can tell people how to live. I know what I'm talking about on this one. I was there.'[6]

He was right – Sinatra and his family were there. Frank claimed his father's side of his family came from Catania in eastern Sicily. But as biographers Anthony Summers and Robbyn Swan demonstrate, he was economical with the truth. Sinatra's family came from the Sicilian town of Lercara Friddi in north west Sicily. This was the birthplace of Salvatore Luciano – better known as Lucky Luciano, one of the founders of the modern Mafia.[7]

Sinatra's father guarded trucks carrying illegal alcohol, and his parents ran an illegal bar during Prohibition. This was the backdrop to Sinatra's adolescence. At private parties

Sinatra loved to tell the following story: 'Marty [his father] once loaned $50 to a guy who ran a bar. When time came for repayment, the debtor simply said he wasn't going to pay, Marty went outside to where the bar owner's horse was tied up. He brought the horse into the bar and shot it dead'.[8]

It wasn't just Sinatra who was attracted by the allure of the gangster. Hollywood made a series of films which immortalised the mob – *Scarface* (1932), *Baby Face* (1933), *Angels With Dirty Faces* (1938), *White Heat* (1949). Major screen stars such as James Cagney and Tony Curtis publicly stated their admiration for the gangster figure. Cagney once said, 'They were kind to us kids. You could only like them. And anyway there was only three ways a kid from my neighbourhood could get ahead. You could become a prizefighter, go into showbusiness or go into crime'.[9] Amid the hardship of the 1930s, the Mafia lifestyle could appear glamorous and exciting. This remains the case today, and leads hip-hop artists to glorify the pimp/gangster lifestyle.

It was hard for people in the entertainment industry to avoid coming into contact with the Mafia – after all, the gangs controlled most nightclubs. This meant musicians and singers were constantly rubbing shoulders with the underworld. But Sinatra's dealings with the Mafia went further than simple admiration and the odd drink. Over recent years a series of books have provided compelling evidence that Sinatra used the Mafia to aid his career and provided help in return.

In 1942 Sinatra signed a contract which released him from the Tommy Dorsey Band. But there was a catch – the deal entitled Dorsey to one third of all Sinatra's earnings above $100 a week for the next ten years, with a further 10 percent to go to Dorsey's manager. Sinatra was desperate to get out of the contract. He begged Dorsey to let him go. But it was only when mobster Willie Moretti made Dorsey an offer he couldn't refuse that the contract was scrapped.

Of course, Sinatra's growing reliance on the Mafia had its roots in his family and their connections. Yet it also came down to survival. He was one of the few major stars who openly backed the left, but during the McCarthy era the left was in tatters and Sinatra's career appeared to be going the same way. His friends in the mob gave him help.

FBI documents show that during Sinatra's lean years gangsters across America booked him to play their clubs. Paul 'Skinny' Darmato booked Sinatra to play in his 500 Club in Atlantic City, Moe Dalitz hired him to sing at the Desert Inn in Las Vegas, Joe Fischetti got him work in Chicago, and so on.[11]

There is a fascinating scene in *The Godfather* in which a man asks Don Corleone for a favour. The Don grants his wish and replies, 'Someday, and that day may never come, I will call upon you to do a service for me'.[12] In the 1950s, as Sinatra's popularity soared and his ability to influence people in high places grew – and you can't get much higher than the US president – the day would come for Sinatra to perform a service for old friends.

Sinatra's revival was largely down to one film – *From Here To Eternity*. A simple story, it was a raw, angry, brutal look at love and military life at an American base on Hawaii in the days leading up to the Japanese attack on Pearl Harbor. Sinatra read the script and was desperate to play the part of Private Angelo Maggio, a tough little grunt who was violent, funny and loveable in equal measure. How Sinatra got the role remains a matter of controversy. Whatever the truth, he played the part with real conviction. Released on 4 August 1953, the film was an instant blockbuster. It won eight Oscars, with Sinatra taking the award for Best Supporting Actor.[1]

Ol' Blue Eyes was back. He had already signed with a new record label, Capitol Records, in March 1953. But it was a standard contract because most music executives were no longer interested in him. Alan Livingstone, vice-president in charge of A&R and sales at Capitol, explained how Sinatra signed with the label: 'Frank and I talked and I signed him to a seven-year contract, one year with six options, which is as long as you can sign anybody. I gave him a standard royalty of 5 percent and gave him a scale advance. He was glad to have a place to make records'.[2]

The development of the Long Player (LP) plastic microgroove record in 1948 had transformed the business of making records. The creation of the 10-inch record allowed artists to record four or five tracks per side. By the mid-1950s the 12-inch version was becoming common, permitting eight songs per side. The development of the LP gave artists greater scope to develop themes and expand on their musical ideas. Sinatra exploited this development to the full.

In 1954 he released his first LP for Capitol Records – *Songs for Young Lovers*. It was an instant sensation, outselling the most popular singles of the day. Produced by Nelson Riddle, it was hailed as fresh and exciting. Sinatra's singing style had become almost conversational, yet it packed an emotional punch few could match. His phrasing was perfect – the epitome of unforced swing. 'Just One Of Those Things' and 'All Of Me' remain two outstanding classics on the album. The moods captured by Sinatra on *Songs For Young Lovers / Swing Easy!* would be developed and bettered on later albums as he revolutionised the art of performing a pop song.[3]

Between 1954 and 1965 Sinatra established himself as an enduring artist of popular culture. He could not have done this without the help of some of the best swing musicians in the world, and a number of inventive and imaginative arrangers and conductors – Nelson Riddle, Billy May and Gordon Jenkins. Riddle remains one of the most famous vocal and musical directors of all time. He and Sinatra recorded 14 albums together, one of the greatest bodies of work in American popular culture.[4] George Jacobs, Sinatra's valet through much of the 1950s and 1960s, said, 'Nelson Riddle helped channel the rage and pain of Sinatra's turbulent thirties…turning the man from the ultimate crooner to something much deeper and stronger, the ultimate stylist.'[5]

Sinatra followed Songs *For Young Lovers / Swing Easy!* with a series of thematically organised albums. His emotional musical vocabulary had grown so large that he had become an artist capable of sustaining a single mood for 16 songs, exploring every variation and graduation. The songs on these albums captured the mood of 1950s America perfectly.

The decade saw the US at the height of an economic boom. The standard of living of working class people rose, and mass production made cars, record players, fridges and televisions affordable to large numbers. Sinatra articulated the optimism of the times in a series of upbeat albums – *A Swingin' Affair* (1957), *Come Fly With Me* (1958), and *Come Dance With Me* (1958). He was creating a new sound, but one which harked back to the era of swing. By the late 1950s many of the musicians Sinatra employed had been playing big band jazz for more than 30 years and were at the pinnacle of their careers.

A Swingin' Affair became a runaway success. It was a

trend-setting record. Sinatra turned his attention to some of the best songs around and made them his own – Cole Porter's 'Night And Day', George and Ira Gershwin's 'Nice Work If You Can Get It' and 'I Got Plenty O' Nuttin', and Duke Ellington's 'I Got It Bad And That Ain't Good'. Sinatra and Riddle's big band arrangements took the concept of romantic swing to new heights.

Come Fly With Me demonstrates the self-belief of the era. It's an album that celebrates Sinatra's jet set, hedonistic lifestyle. Such a life was just a dream for most of Sinatra's fans, but increasing living standards meant an increasing number of people could take an annual two-week holiday in the sun. Billy May's orchestra created a bold, brash and brassy sound, and the album sounded great on the new hi-fi sets millions of Americans were buying. *Come Dance With Me* followed in a similar vein. Again May created a sound firmly rooted in the big band era. Sinatra noted, 'Working with Billy May is like having a bucket of cold water thrown in your face'.[6]

Yet on albums such as *In The Wee Small Hours* (1955), *Only The Lonely* (1958) and *No One Cares* (1959), Sinatra captured the other side of post-war America – the alienation of city life, the loneliness, displacement and neurosis. Again he was in tune with his audience. The bobbysoxers of the 1940s had grown up – many now had their own families and, like Sinatra, had experienced the highs and lows of married life. Many were all too aware that love and marriage did not necessarily go together like a 'horse and carriage'. Songs like 'The Night We Called It A Day', 'Good Bye' and 'Can't We

Be Friends' expressed the pain of separation and the hurt when a relationship ends.

In The Wee Small Hours is one of the greatest vocal albums ever recorded. Sinatra's naked emotional intensity climbed peaks never reached before. The 16 songs are about unrequited love and loneliness. Almost all were recorded when Sinatra knew his marriage to Ava was finished. Sinatra did not write the songs, but his interpretations made them intensely personal. As John Collis writes, 'The title song defines the parameters of the project, and at last we can see this is Sinatra's own version of the blues, his own expression of soul'.[7]

The album *Only The Lonely* takes Sinatra on another even darker journey of despair – the relationship with Gardner was over and there was no going back. On the track 'One For My Baby', Sinatra sang:

It's a quarter to three,
There's no one in the place except you and me
So set them up Joe,
I've got a little story I think you should know
We're drinking my friend, to the end of a brief episode
Make it one for my baby
And one more for the road.

No bar room song has been sung better. Riddle called *Only The Lonely* 'the best vocal album I've ever done'. He wrote the orchestrations at a time of great personal tragedy. Both his daughter and mother had just died. Riddle said, 'If one can attach events like that to music, perhaps *Only The Lonely* was the result'.[8]

On the album *No One Cares* Sinatra teamed up with Gordon Jenkins, who he had worked with on *Where Are You?* in 1957. The sound remains melancholic and moody, but Sinatra's vocals convey a sense of resignation at a love lost. Broken-down cottages and the weather are used as metaphors for a failed relationship. It's all cheery stuff! But the three of these albums see an artist at the height of his expressive power, and the combination of brass and strings create wonderful, windswept soundscapes.

In between these albums Sinatra recorded *Songs for Swingin' Lovers* (1956), another collaboration with Riddle on which they seemed to be pushing each other to ever greater musical heights. The theme of the album is the joy of being in love. It is crammed full of classics – 'You Make Me Feel So Young', 'Old Devil Moon', 'Anything Goes' and 'Makin' Whoopee'. But its greatest song is 'I've Got You Under My Skin'. Everyone knows it and many will have heard it 100 times, but it is a song you never tire of hearing. Many argue *Songs For Swingin' Lovers* is the definitive Sinatra album – and it's a hard claim to refute.

Following the success of *From Here to Eternity*, Sinatra made further films. In fact, between 1954 and 1955 he made more movies than any other star in Hollywood. Like his music, Sinatra's choice of films reflected US society. There were vibrant, confident musicals such as *High Society* (1956) and *Pal Joey* (1957), and films which reflected a darker side of America. *The Man with the Golden Arm* (1955) dealt with drug addiction at a time when this was rarely discussed, while *The Manchurian Candidate* (1962) is a political thriller which shows a society haunted by the effects of the Cold War.

Songs For Swingin' Lovers was released in the same year that Elvis Presley stormed the charts with 'Heartbreak Hotel' – Presley's first number one single. Sinatra didn't like Elvis and said so: 'By means of its almost imbecilic reiteration and sly, lewd, in plain fact, dirty lyrics rock and roll manages to be martial music of every sideburned delinquent on the face of the earth'.[9]

I detect just a hint of jealousy here. You have to admire Sinatra's hypocrisy – his stage act was based on sexual innuendo. But for now Sinatra was on top of the world. It was reported that in 1957 Sinatra earned $4 million, making him the highest paid entertainer in the history of showbusiness. But that wasn't enough. Sinatra wanted to be in an even bigger league – he wanted to be a kingmaker in politics.

Frank at Carnegie Hall performing a benefit for Martin Luther King's Southern Christian Leadership Conference.

08 / Anything goes: the Rat Pack

 By 1960 there was a new mood of optimism in America. The economy was booming, McCarthyism seemed like a bad nightmare, the Civil Rights Movement was beating back the racists in the Jim Crow South, and few Americans spared a thought for Vietnam. To top it all, a debonair Democratic Party candidate for president named John F Kennedy (JFK) promised the dawn of a new era.

In this giddy atmosphere, nightclubs and casinos flourished. One US city became synonymous with this culture of hedonism – Las Vegas. Its bright lights drew millions who were encouraged to spend, spend, spend. You could catch a show, feed your money to the hungry slot machines and dine out on 'surf and turf'. The king of this gambling mecca was Frank Sinatra, and his courtiers were the Rat Pack – Dean

Martin, Sammy Davis Jr, Peter Lawford and Joey Bishop.[1]

Dean Martin was famous before he met Sinatra. His comedy partnership with Jerry Lewis had already made him a star. After the duo split, Sinatra got Martin one of his first film roles in *Some Came Running* in 1958. The favour cemented their friendship.

Sammy Davis Jr was a successful singer in his own right. In the mid-1940s Sinatra had invited Sammy and the drummer Buddy Rich to see him perform at the world-famous Copacabana Club in New York. The doorman refused the pair entry because Davis was black. When Sinatra found out he tore a strip off the club manager and the doorman. He invited Sammy back to the club. This time Davis was let in and, for good measure, Sinatra had his friends sit with the young entertainer – the colour bar was broken.[2]

Some of the Rat Pack. First four from the left – Sammy Davis Jr, Frank, Dean Martin and Peter Lawford

Joey Bishop was a moderately successful comedian, and Peter Lawford was a minor Hollywood actor. But in 1954 Lawford had married Patricia Kennedy. When his brother in law decided to run for president, Frank decided to draw Lawford into his inner circle.

Every year Sinatra and his gang would decamp to Las Vegas to perform and live it up at the Sands Casino and Hotel. FBI files list the Sands as a Mafia-sponsored operation. Sinatra was a sleeping partner.[3] Mafia leaders used him to encourage showbusiness friends to perform at their clubs. He was a willing accomplice – it was time to pay past debts.

Life was one long party for Frank's Rat Pack. They celebrated non-conformity, heavy drinking and practical jokes, and enjoyed being vaguely connected to liberal values. Sinatra's liberal attitudes were made perfectly clear in an interview he gave to *Playboy* magazine:

'Playboy: In combating Communist expansion into underdeveloped areas here and abroad, what can we do except to offer massive material aid and guidance of the kind we've been providing since the end of World War Two?
Sinatra: I don't know. I'm no economist. I don't pretend to have much background in political science. But I do know this much. Attending rallies sponsored by 100 percent anti-Communist cultists or donning white sheets and riding with the Klan – the one that's spelled with a "K" – isn't the answer. All I know is that a nation with our standard of living, with our Social Security system, TVA, farm parity, health plans and unemployment insurance can afford to address itself to the cancers of starvation, substandard housing, educational voids and second class citizenship that still exist in many backsliding areas of our won country. When we've cleaned up these blemishes, then we can go out with a clean conscience to see where else in the world we can help. Hunger is inexcusable in a world where grain rots in silos and butter turns rancid while being held for favourable commodity indices.'

But most of all the Rat Pack liked to portray themselves as the epitome of cool. Their shows were ramshackle affairs – a mix of slapstick humor and song which included crude sexist and racist jokes. It was a world away from Sinatra's anti-racist stance of the 1940s. But he was no longer hanging around with the left – his new friends were the cocktails set.

The real partying began when the crowds went back to their hotel rooms. Sinatra and his entourage made sure festivities lasted long into the next morning. Drink and showgirls were on tap. Women were used, abused and discarded like empty packets of cigarettes.

The high life cost money, and the money earned by the Rat Pack at the Sands was not enough. Films were a quick and easy way of making a dollar and keeping the Rat Pack together. Sinatra had a five-year plan – to make a movie a year. *Ocean's 11*, *Sergeants 3*, *4 for Texas*, *Robin and the 7 Hoods* and *Marriage on the Rocks* followed. They were quickly made and of varying quality, ranging from the OK to the terrible. Probably the best was *Ocean's 11*, which the *New York Times* objected to on the grounds that it left audiences rooting for the crooks![4]

JFK had seen the Rat Pack perform at the Sands while they were filming *Ocean's 11*. As a Democrat, Sinatra supported JFK. But there was more to it than just admiration. JFK was a man who was going places and had real power – this was someone Sinatra wanted to rub shoulders with. For his part, JFK was fascinated by Sinatra. He loved the glamour of Hollywood, the women and the celebrity lifestyle. The pair struck up a friendship. Sinatra even acted as a pimp, providing young women for Kennedy. Frank made sure the senator was well-supplied with showgirls and prostitutes whenever he was in Las Vegas or California. Sinatra also introduced Judith

Cambell (her married name was Exner) to JFK. Later it would be revealed that, while sleeping with JFK, Campbell was a lover of the mobster Sam Giancana. She acted as a go-between, passing information about a joint CIA/Mafia plan to assassinate Fidel Castro.[5] FBI documents also show the Mafia used Sinatra to gain access to JFK.[6]

Kennedy and his supporters liked to cultivate a liberal image. Of course, compared with later US presidents Kennedy does appear liberal. But as a senator in the 1950s he did not speak out against the McCarthyite witch-hunts. And when he became president Kennedy took the world to the brink of nuclear destruction during the Cuban missile crisis and doubled the number of US troops in Vietnam.

When Kennedy announced he was going to stand for the presidency in 1960, Sinatra rechristened his gang the 'Jack Pack' and cajoled *Frank with* every member to back JFK. He took Jimmy Van Heusen's song *JFK* 'High Hopes' and, with the help of Sammy Cahn, reworked the lyrics to turn it into JFK's official campaign song:

K-E-double-N-E-D-Y,
Jack's the nation's favorite guy.
Everyone wants to back Jack,
Jack is on the right track.
And he's got HIGH HOPES
High apple-pie in the sky hopes

The 'Jack Pack' turned up in force at the Democratic National Convention in July. Sinatra also used his connections to persuade other stars to endorse JFK at the rally – Shirley MacLaine, Angie Dickinson, Janet Lee, Tony Curtis and Judy Garland. But some delegates from Mississippi booed and heckled Sammy Davis Jr, calling him a 'nigger' and a 'freak'.[7] These racists not only opposed him because he was black, they were outraged that he was engaged to a white actress. Davis was so angry and humiliated that he stormed off the stage.

It was around this time that Sinatra decided to take on the witch-hunters and right-wing zealots once more. He announced he would make a film called *The Execution of Private Slovik*. It would tell the story of the only American executed by the US army for desertion during the Second World War. Sinatra hired Albert Maltz, one of the Hollywood Ten, to write the script. He knew Maltz from the time they made *The House I Live In*. Since then, Maltz had been imprisoned, fined and blacklisted for refusing to answer questions put by the House Un-American Activities Committee. The only explanation for Sinatra's decision to hire Maltz was that he was out to break the blacklist. Maltz himself wrote, 'I had not worked on a film in Hollywood since 1948 and I, like others who were on the blacklist, kept hoping that the blacklist would be broken, so to receive Frank's call in 1960 was enormously exciting to me. He anticipated all the problems and the outcry from the American Legion types, but he said he didn't care. He wanted to break the blacklist'.[8]

John Wayne, the man famous for his cowboy films and ultra-patriotic politics, entered the fray to ask, 'I wonder how Sinatra's crony, Senator John Kennedy, feels about him hiring such a man? I'd like to know his attitude because he is the one who is making plans to run the government of our country'.[9] Sinatra fired back with full-page ads in the Hollywood trade papers defending his decision to hire Maltz. He was not going to back down. The right-wing press was apoplectic, but Frank would not budge. In Washington, a Senate investigative committee was set up to look into attempts by 'Communists' to infiltrate the motion picture industry. Sinatra brushed that off as well.

Prior to announcing he would make *The Execution of Private Slovik*, Sinatra had signed an advertising contract with General Motors worth $250,000. The company threatened to pull out if Sinatra did not sack Maltz. Frank's reply was, 'Fuck 'em.' Across the country Catholic priests used their pulpits to sermonise against Frank. But even god's ambassadors could not make him back down.

Then Sinatra received a call from someone with more authority – JFK's father. He told Sinatra that hiring Maltz would cost Kennedy the election. 'It's either Maltz or us,' he said.[10] The next day, Sinatra issued the following statement: 'In view of the reaction of my family and friends and the American public I have instructed my attorneys to make a settlement with Albert Maltz and to inform him that he will not write the screenplay for *The Execution of Private Slovik*.'

Sinatra abandoned the idea of directing or producing the

film. He paid Maltz's agent $75,000 – the full cost of the script. But he was too embarrassed to call the writer to explain. George Jacobs, Frank's valet, described how Sinatra reacted to his enforced climbdown: 'He went on a three-day Jack Daniel's binge and totally destroyed his office at Bowmont House. "Who gives a shit? I'm outta this fucking business" he screamed, ripping up books, scripts and hurling over bookcases'.[11] Sinatra even tried to pick a fight with John Wayne at a charity benefit concert.[12]

The election was a straight fight between JFK and Richard Nixon for the Republican Party. Nixon wasn't called Tricky Dicky for nothing. He was a Cold War warrior, who had made his name in the HUAC. Sinatra raised hundreds of thousands of dollars for JFK's campaign, and sang and spoke at a large number of rallies. Almost 69 million Americans cast their vote on polling day in November 1960, and Kennedy won with a majority of just 113,057.

Two nights before JFK's inauguration, Sinatra was invited to a party hosted by Kennedy, where he sat at the head of the table next to the new president. As one of Sinatra's biographers notes, 'A month after his 45th birthday, it seemed, he not only had fame and fortune but entrée at the pinnacle of political power'.[13]

The inauguration was a star-studded affair. But one of the Jack Pack was not welcome. JFK's personal assistant phoned Sammy Davis Jr and said the president did not want him there. The assistant told Davis his presence might jeopardise JFK's goals in regards to equality. Kennedy was worried Sammy's relationship with a white woman would upset white racists – such was the level of JFK's commitment to the struggle for civil rights.

The night before the inauguration Sinatra presided over a gala showbiz tribute to Kennedy. The stars who performed included Sidney Poitier, Ella Fitzgerald, Nat 'King' Cole and Harry Belafonte. Dean Martin and Sammy Davis Jr didn't show.[14]

Shortly after the election, Kennedy announced he was going to spend the weekend in Palm Springs. Sinatra was overjoyed. JFK's office indicated the president would like to stay at Frank's home, so he had a heliport and new guest-house built for the president and his entourage. Then shortly before JFK was due to arrive, Sinatra was told the president would be staying at the home of one of his neighbours – Bing Crosby, a lifelong Republican and supporter of Nixon. Sinatra was devastated. It was the ultimate snub and a public humiliation for a man who had done everything he could to get JFK elected.

Why did Kennedy humiliate Sinatra? A simple explanation is that the Kennedy family used and abused everyone. Their goal was the White House, and they would use anyone to get there. But there were other reasons. JFK's brother, Bobby, wanted to declare war on organised crime. So it was a touch embarrassing that the president and Sinatra had been cavorting with well known gangsters and their lovers. Sinatra's connection with the underworld meant he was too hot to handle.

The political rug may have been pulled from under Sinatra's feet, but his career was still on an upward trajectory.

Throughout the 1960s Sinatra was successful on many fronts. He remained the consummate performer. He invested his money in casinos and film-making. And in December 1960 he announced he was going to launch his own record company, Reprise Records. The name matched the company's slogan: 'Records you'll want to play again and again'. Sinatra wanted to give himself and other artists who signed to the label the rights to their own material. A number of artists signed up, including Dean Martin, Count Basie, Nancy Sinatra and Bing Crosby.

Sinatra would record almost 30 albums for Reprise and Warner Reprise in the 1960s – a staggering number by any standards. Many of them were of high quality. *Ring-A-Ding Ding!* (1960) was the first album released on the label, and it shows Sinatra in a cocky mood – it's finger-snapping jazz at its best. Sinatra also recorded three albums with the Count Basie Orchestra: *Sinatra-Basie* (1963), *It Might As Well Be Swing* (1964) and the glorious *Sinatra At The Sands* (1966). The combined talents of Sinatra and one of the greatest big bands in history are enough to take your breath away. All three albums are a riot of sound and vocal dexterity. *Sinatra-Basie* spawned the mighty 'Nice Work If You Can Get It' and '(Love Is) The Tender Trap'. *It Might As Well Be Swing* gave the world the awesome 'Fly Me To The Moon'. But the best was definitely saved till last. *Sinatra At The Sands* is a stunning performance, with all the classic Sinatra songs. 'Come Fly With Me', 'It Was A Very Good Year', 'One For My Baby' and a host of others are given the atomic Basie treatment.

Sinatra's voice was as strong as ever, but Reprise was fast going into debt. In 1963 Sinatra was forced to sell two thirds of the company to Warner Brothers. It gave him a cheque for $1 million and the joint company went on releasing Sinatra albums.

Frank continued to oppose racism, and in 1961 and 1963 he appeared at Carnegie Hall to perform benefits for Martin Luther King's Southern Christian Leadership Conference. He also donated money to the National Association for the Advancement of Colored People (NAACP) throughout the 1950s and 1960s.[15]

Martin Luther King

It was during this period that Sinatra returned to his most majestic anti-racist songs – 'Ol' Man River' and 'Lost In the Stars'. Both can be found on the album *The Concert Sinatra* (1963). The power of these songs is reinforced when you remember that 1963 was the year King won a major battle against segregation in Birmingham, Alabama. It was also the year King made his famous 'I Have A Dream' speech in Washington. The musicologist Will Friedwald noted that Sinatra may have been almost 50 years old at this time, but his voice was still on top form. 'His top note would be the high F he hits on '(Love Is) The Tender Trap', going down to the ultra deep Jolsonian low G on 'Ol' Man River'. That amounts to a span of nearly two octaves'.[16]

Then, on 22 November 1963, President Kennedy was

assassinated. Bit by bit, Frank's world turned upside down. His hatred for the Republican Party appeared as strong as before. At his concerts, Sinatra adapted the words to 'The Lady Is A Tramp' to sing 'She hates California, it's Reagan and damp...that's why the Lady is a tramp'. But politics was moving at a pace. People were taking to the streets. The Civil Rights Movement turned into Black Power and urban revolts. The anti Vietnam War movement radicalised a generation of political activists, and gave birth to the women's movement and the campaign for gay and lesbian rights.

In 1968, Nixon won the presidential election, promising to end the war in Vietnam. Sinatra came out in support of the Democrats in the election, but his support was half-hearted. His tired sexist and racist jokes may have appealed to older, more conservative audiences, but they left most people cold – especially the radicalised younger generation.

Sinatra's musical supremacy was also challenged. Soul, rock and funk music spoke to the young in a way Sinatra could only dream of. His sound was dated, and becoming bombastic and pompous. Instead of setting musical trends, he was forced to copy them. His musical output became increasingly erratic. There were still great albums and songs – 'Strangers In The Night' and 'Send In The Clowns' were big hits in 1966. But albums such as *Cycles* (1968) and *Watertown* (1969) were cliche-ridden affairs trying to come to terms with modern pop songs.

Sinatra was losing his touch. He was no longer the king. Mick Jagger was cool, Marvin Gaye had soul power and Jim Morrison was a rebel. To the 1968 generation, Sinatra dressed like their dads, had the same politics as their dads and was about as cool as their dads.

Sinatra ended the 1960s with the release of *My Way*, a relatively weak album that didn't even reach the top 20 of the album charts. However, it did spawn the monster single 'My Way' (1969). The song is a justification of the American Dream – the idea that everyone can succeed if they work hard. But it provokes another reaction in most audiences – a mood of sadness, regret and melancholy. Why? Because most working class people don't do it their way – life is one long struggle, and the deck is always loaded against them. These twin responses explain the extraordinary power of the song.

By now, Sinatra looked as though he came from another era. In June 1971 he announced his retirement. At a farewell performance, he made 'Angel Eyes' his final song. On the last line, 'Excuse me while I disappear', the spotlight went out and Sinatra was gone.

'Excuse me while I disappear' – the spotlight went out and Sinatra was gone

09 / Nancy: the Reagan years

In 1970, Sinatra shocked everyone, including many of his friends, when he announced he was going to back the Republican Ronald Reagan for governor of California. The declaration came in typical, uncompromising fashion: 'I support the man, not the party any more. If people don't like that, screw them... Reagan is an outstanding candidate...a very honest guy who believes what he does'.[1]

Outstanding? Honest? Who was Sinatra trying to kid? Reagan was a reactionary of the first order. He had been a friendly witness for the HUAC and named many of Sinatra's close friends and colleagues. He supported the death penalty and was a racist pig. In 1962, Reagan said of America's black population, 'In their own country, they're eating each other for lunch'.[2]

Sinatra returned to politics and made friends among a new class of gangsters – the Republican Party. The million-dollar question is: why did he do it? There is no simple answer. Sinatra did not suddenly lurch to the right – it was a long, drawn-out process. He had wealth and fame beyond most people's dreams. Bit by bit it distorted his view of the world and of himself.

Sinatra had always been a contradictory character. In the 1940s he had backed the left yet at the same time built links with the Mafia. In the 1950s and 1960s he was one of the key musical supporters of the Civil Rights Movement, yet he made racist jokes on stage.

Even when he came out in support of Reagan for governor, Sinatra opposed much of what Reagan stood for. He condemned Reagan's plans to cut $10 million in aid for the elderly, blind and disabled in California, and when Reagan opposed the right to abortion, Sinatra came out publicly in defence of a woman's right to choose. But the Democratic Party had betrayed him and the left he knew in his youth had been smashed. He was on a trajectory towards the Republicans.

JFK may not have stayed at Sinatra's house, but there were plenty of Republicans prepared to grace his table. Spiro Agnew and Ronald Reagan were regular guests at Sinatra's Palm Springs home. Agnew had shocked people during a tour of Detroit in the 1968 election campaign when he had exclaimed, 'If you've seen one city slum you've seen them all'.[3] But when Nixon tried to dump Agnew in the 1972 election, Sinatra had come to his rescue with a fresh adaptation of 'The Lady is a Tramp' as Agnew's campaign song: 'The Gentleman is a Tramp'. Agnew was no gentleman. The Maryland senator had been taking bribes from building contractors since 1967 and was forced to resign in October 1973. The more Sinatra hung around such characters the more he began to ape them.

The contradictions in Sinatra's life grew wider until, in April 1973, he resolved them by nailing his colours firmly to the Republican mast. Nixon asked Sinatra to sing at the White House. One of the songs he asked Sinatra to perform was 'The House I Live In'. The irony was not lost on some – one of the great songs of the Popular Front era was being sung to one of the movement's most vicious opponents. But any song that survives its historical beginnings can be turned into its opposite. I remember reviewing 'White Riot' by The Clash many years ago and claiming it was 'revolutionary pop'. Twenty years later it was being used as a soundtrack for a toilet paper commercial! By now Sinatra didn't care. He was where he always wanted to be – a White House insider.

His retirement didn't last long – two years to be precise. The voice may have begun to lose the elasticity of his youth – after all, he was nearing 60 years of age – but his greatest vocal strength, his precise and measured phrasing, remained.

From 1974 until his death Sinatra rarely entered the recording studio, and when he did the results were not impressive. He often chose 'modern' pop songs, which clearly did not suit his singing style. More and more, Sinatra relied on the reissue of past albums and greatest hit packages.

However, his live performances continued to draw crowds around the world. In 1975 he performed 140 concerts to more than 500,000 people. [4]

Sinatra spent the second half of 1979 working on an ambitious musical project entitled 'Trilogy'. The concept behind the triple album was simple. The first album, *The Past*, sees Sinatra and producer Billy May revisit some of the great standards of popular American culture. The second disc is a mixed bag, with songs which cover the entire rock era. The final album, *The Future*, is unbearable, pretentious nonsense.

Ronald Reagan stood for the presidency in 1980 and Sinatra agreed to campaign and raise funds. He contributed $4 million of his own money.[5] Just as he had for JFK, Sinatra organised an inaugural gala for Reagan. This time all the Hollywood reactionaries were there – Bob Hope, Marie Osmond, Charlton Heston. Sinatra claimed it was a star-studded gala! But when it came to the inauguration, Sinatra discovered he was not among the 100 chosen to stand on the steps of the US Capitol as the president was sworn in. Once again Sinatra's unsavoury connections had come back to haunt him. But this time Sinatra simply marched up to the steps and joined the others. His smiling face is captured on the official White House photograph. [6]

Reagan's administration wasted no time in seeking to overcome the impact of the US defeat in Vietnam, which had become known as the 'Vietnam syndrome'. It ordered the invasions of Grenada and Panama, it supported the murderous right-wing Contras in Nicaragua, and it blockaded Cuba. Reagan and his friend Margaret Thatcher pursued their free market economic policies, wealth gushed to the top of society, and being filthy rich became something to boast about. Sinatra obliged his friends with his patriotic anthems, 'My Way' and 'New York, New York'. But for many, the 1980s passed into memory as a time of high unemployment and union bashing.

It is too depressing to catalogue Sinatra's rabid proclamations during the 1980s. One ten-night musical engagement demonstrates just how far to the right he had travelled. In 1981 he played Sun City, the playground for South African whites during the apartheid era. The artist who had done as much as anyone to champion civil rights in the US in the 1940s and 1950s was now prepared to endorse one of the most disgusting regimes in the world.

But ten years later, completely out of the blue, Sinatra took one more swipe at racism. He wrote an article for the *Los Angeles Times* entitled 'The Haters and Bigots Will be Judged'. In it he argued:

'We are created equal! No one of us is better than any one of us! That's the headline proclaimed in 1776 and inscribed across centuries in the truth of the ages. Those inspired words from the Declaration of Independence mock bigotry and anti-Semitism. Then why do I still hear race and colour haters spewing their poisons? Why do I still flinch at innuendoes of venom and inequality? Why do innocent children still grow up to be despised? Why do haters' jokes still get big laughs when passed in whispers from scum to scum? You know the ones I mean – the 'Some of my best friends are Jewish…' crowd.

'As for those others, those cross-burning bigots to whom mental slavery is alive and well, I don't envy their trials in the next world, where their thoughts and words and actions will be judged by a jury of one...

'And when the music fades, think of the guts of Rosa Parks, who by a single act in a single moment changed America as much as anyone else who lived. I'm no angel. I've had my moments. I've done a few things in my life of which I'm not too proud, but I have never unloved a human being because of race, creed or colour'.[7]

What inspired Sinatra to write the article? Was he making one last stand against racism or was it just fear of his own mortality? I think it was a combination of both. In 1990 his Rat Pack accomplice Sammy Davis Jr had died and Sinatra was feeling the effects of old age.

He was forgetting his lines and cues on stage and, in March 1994, he collapsed from exhaustion during a concert. The following December Sinatra announced his retirement from live performance. He released a couple of worthy albums – *Duets* and *Duets II* – on which 'icons' such as Barbara Streisland, Anita Baker, Neil Diamond, Bono, Kenny G and Julio Inglesias recorded some of the classic Sinatra hits. Interestingly, these worthies and Sinatra never sang together in person – the vocals were all spliced together in the recording studio.

By now, TV news programmes and newspapers were preparing their Sinatra obituaries. And he didn't disappoint them. On 14 May 1998 Frank Sinatra died.

In Las Vegas, the casinos turned off their neon lights for a minute's tribute. In New York, the Empire State Building was lit blue. Thousands packed Times Square to say their farewells, and radio stations around the world played Sinatra's songs into the night. It was the perfect tribute to a musical legend.

But the last word should go to the man who, towards the end of his life, finished every concert by telling his audience, 'May you live a hundred years, and may the last voice you hear be mine.'

Notes

01 / I've got you under my skin

1   For a comprehensive guide to Sinatra's film and recorded work, there is no finer discography than John Ridgway's monumental guide *Sinatrafile* Part 2 and Part 3 (Birmingham, 1991).

2   Nancy Sinatra, *Frank Sinatra 1915-1998: An American Legend* (New York, 1998), p176.

3   Kitty Kelley, *His Way: The Unauthorized Biography of Frank Sinatra* (London, 1986), p115.

4   Duke Ellington, *Music Is My Mistress* (London, 1974).

02/ You make me feel so young: the early years

1   Pete Hamill, *Why Sinatra Matters* (Boston, 2003), pp38-39.

2   Howard Zinn, *A People's History of the United States* (London, 1996), p247.

3   Pete Hamill, *Why Sinatra Matters*, p45.

4   John Egerton, *Speak Now Against The Day* (New York, 1995), p123.

5   Gerald Mayer, 'Frank Sinatra: The Popular Front and an American Icon', *Science and Society* (New York), Fall 2002, p2.

6   Seymour Hersh, *The Dark Side of Camelot* (New York), p139.

7   Anthony Summers and Robbyn Swan, *Sinatra: The Life* (London, 2005), p19.

8   *Photoplay* (New York), October 1945.

9   Howard Zinn, *A People's History of the United States*, p383.

10   Pete Hamill, *Why Sinatra Matters*, p38.

11   Will Friedwald, *Sinatra: The Song is You* (New York, 1995), p87.

12   TV mini-series *Sinatra* (1992).

13   Connie Haines, *For Once in my Life* (New York, 1976), p127.

03/   It all came true: the bobbysox years

1   Kitty Kelley, *His Way*, p74.

2   Stanislas G Pugliese (ed), *Frank Sinatra: History, Identity and Italian American Culture* (London, 2004), p74.

3   Lawrence J Quirk and William Schoell, *The Rat Pack: Neon Nights With The Kings Of Cool* (Dallas, 2002), p27.

4   Nancy Sinatra, *Frank Sinatra*, p55.

5   Phil Hardy and David Laing, *The Faber Companion To 20th Century Popular Music* (London, 1990).

6   Will Friedwald, *Sinatra*, p122.

7   Eric Hobsbawm, *Age Of Extremes: The Short Twentieth Century 1914-1991* (London, 1994), p328.

8   Anthony Summers and Robbyn Swan, *Sinatra: The Life*, p91.

9   Radio interview with Paul Compton, KGIL, San Francisco, 5 June 1970.

10   Figures obtained from Columbia Records press department.

04/   The house I live in: Frank and the Popular Front

1   Kitty Kelley, *His Way* , p101.

2   Stanislas G Pugliese (ed), *Frank Sinatra*, p51; Kitty Kelley, *His Way*, p102.

3   *New York Times*, 1 November 1944.

4   Howard Zinn, *A People's History of the United States*, p391.

5   Fraser M Ottanelli, *The Communist Party Of The United States From The Depression to World War 2* (New Jersey, 1991), p154.

6   Foreign Language Publishing House, *Communist International: Seventh Congress of the Communist International*.

7   Fraser M Ottanelli, *The Communist Party Of The United States*, p179.

8   Michael Denning, *The Cultural Front* (London, 1996), pxix.

9   *Look Magazine*, 8 August 1947

10   Kitty Kelley, *His Way*, p115.

11   Patrick McGilligan and Paul Buhle, *Tender Comrades* (New York, 1997), p617.

12   Stanislas G Pugliese (ed), *Frank Sinatra*, p25.

13   Kitty Kelley, *His Way*, p115.

14   Nancy Sinatra, *Frank Sinatra*, p68.

15   Anthony Summers and Robbyn Swan, *Sinatra: The Life*, p113.

16   David Margolick, *Strange Fruit: Billie Holiday, Café Society, and an Early Cry for Civil Rights* (London, 2000), p27.

17   Gerald Mayer, 'Frank Sinatra: The Popular Front and an American Icon'.

18   Michael Denning, *The Cultural Front*, p70.

19   Anthony Summers and Robbyn Swan, *Sinatra: The Life*, p111.

20   Gerald Mayer, 'Frank Sinatra: The Popular Front and an American Icon'; *Daily Worker*; *PM*.

21   Gerald Mayer, 'Frank Sinatra: The Popular Front and an American Icon'.

22   Kitty Kelley, *His Way*.

23   Kitty Kelley, *His Way*, pp117, 118.

24   Will Friedwald, *Sinatra*, p23.

05/ When no one cares: the bad years

1   Chris Harman, *A People's History of the World* (London, 1999), p546.

2   Howard Zinn, *A People's History of the United States*, p428.

3   A M Sperber and Eric Lax, *Bogart* (London, 1998), p359; Gerald Mayer, 'Frank Sinatra: The Popular Front and an American Icon'.

4   Gerald Mayer, 'Frank Sinatra: The Popular Front and an American Icon'.

5   A M Sperber and Eric Lax, *Bogart*, p368.

6   Victor Navasky, *Naming Names*, p80; A M Sperber and Eric Lax, *Bogart*, pp372-383.

7   Kitty Kelley, *His Way*, p120.

8   'Why I Came To Washington', *Washington Daily News*, 10 December 1947.

9   Chris Rojek, *Frank Sinatra* (Cambridge, 2004), p18.

10   Stanislas G Pugliese (ed), *Frank Sinatra*, p52; Kitty Kelley, *His Way*, p119.

11   Kenneth Goff, *Red Betrayal Of Youth* (1948).

12   Tom Kuntz and Phil Kuntz, *The Sinatra Files: The Life Of An American Icon Under Government Surveillance* (New York, 2000), pxi; Stanislas G Pugliese (ed), *Frank Sinatra*, p176.

13   Kitty Kelley, *His Way*, p120.

14   Tom Kuntz and Phil Kuntz, *The Sinatra Files*, pp61-66.

15   Gerald Mayer, 'Frank Sinatra: The Popular Front and an American Icon'.

16   George Lipsitz, *Rainbow At Midnight: Labour and Culture in the 1940s* (New York, 1994), p203; Gerald Mayer, 'Frank Sinatra: The Popular Front and an American Icon'.

17   Chris Rojek, *Frank Sinatra*, p98.

18   Patrick McGilligan and Paul Buhle, *Tender Comrades*, p412.

19   Will Friedwald, *Sinatra*, p166.

06/   Mack the Knife: the Mafia

1   *The Godfather* (Paramount, 1972).

2   Many thanks to Tom Behan for his useful comments on the growth of the Mafia in Sicily.

3   Anthony Summers and Robbyn Swan, *Sinatra: The Life*, p6.

4   *The Mafia: The First Hundred Years* (London, 1993), pp295-303.

5   'Al Capone and the St Valentine's Day Massacre', mysterynet.com.

6   Pete Hamill, *Why Sinatra Matters*, p74.

7   Anthony Summers and Robbyn Swan, *Sinatra: The Life*, p7.

8   Michael Munn, *Sinatra: The Untold Story* (London 2003), p10.

9   Michael Munn, *Sinatra: The Untold Story*, p12.

10   Tom Kuntz and Phil Kuntz, *The Sinatra Files*, pp93-119; Kitty Kelley, *His Way*, p172

11   One of the biggest controversies surrounding Sinatra's career is how he managed to obtain the role of Private Maggio in *From Here To Eternity*. Again most biographers of Sinatra agree that in one way or another Sinatra did get help from his friends in the Mafia.

12   *The Godfather*.

07/ It was a very good year: the revival

1   Ethlie Ann Vare (ed), *Legend: Frank Sinatra and the American Dream* (New York, 1995), pp61-63.

2   Will Friedwald, *Sinatra*, p206.

3   Because the sales of *Songs For Young Lovers* were so good Riddle and Sinatra went back into the recording studio, re-recorded the album and added eight further songs. The result was *Swing Easy*.

4   The key Sinatra / Riddle collaborations are *Songs For Young Lovers* (1953), *Swing Easy* (1954), *In The Wee Small Hours* (1955), *Songs For Swingin' Lovers!* (1955-56), *Close To You* (1956), *A Swingin' Affair* (1956), *Only The Lonely* (1958), *Nice 'n' Easy* (1960), *Sinatra's Swingin' Sessions* (1960), *The Concert Sinatra* (1963), *Sinatra's Sinatra* (1963), *The Days Of Wine And Roses* (1964), *Strangers In The Night* (1966) and *Moonlight Sinatra* (1966).

5   George Jacobs and William Stadiem, *Mr S: The Last Word On Frank Sinatra* (London 2004), p58.

6   Quoted by Pete Welding on the sleave notes from the album *Come Dance With Me*.

7   John Collis, *The Complete Guide To The Music Of Frank Sinatra* (London, 1998).

8   Will Friedwald, *Sinatra*, pp246-247.

9   Richard Iton, *Solidarity Blues: Race, Culture And The American Left* (London, 2000), p293.

08/ Anything goes: the Rat Pack
1   The original 'Rat Pack' was an informal association founded in 1955 and presided over by Humphrey Bogart – Lauren Bacall coined the term. Original members of Bogart's 'Rat Pack' included Lauren Bacall, David Niven, Judy Garland and songwriter Jimmy Van Heusen. Frank Sinatra was inducted as a cub member soon after it was launched.
2   Lawrence J Quirk and William Schoell, *The Rat Pack*, p101.
3   FBI files list the Sands Casino and Cal-Neva Lodge as Mafia-controlled fronts. Sinatra had major shareholdings in both venues.
4   Lawrence J Quirk and William Schoell, *The Rat Pack*, p189.
5   Anthony Summers and Robbyn Swan, *Sinatra: The Life*, p265; Judith Exner, *My Story* (New York, 1977).
6   Tom Kuntz and Phil Kuntz, *The Sinatra Files*, pp120-149.
7   Lawrence J Quirk and William Schoell, *The Rat Pack*, p196.
8   Kitty Kelley, *His Way*, p297.
9   Kitty Kelley, *His Way*, p298.
10   Tom Kuntz and Phil Kuntz, *The Sinatra Files*, p131.
11   George Jacobs and William Stadiem, *Mr S*, p145.
12   Michael Munn, *Sinatra: The Untold Story*, p208.
13   Anthony Summers and Robbyn Swan, *Sinatra: The Life*, p279.
14   To be fair Poitier, Fitzgerald, Cole and Belafonte were unaware of what had happened to Sammy.
15   Gerald Mayer, 'Frank Sinatra: The Popular Front and an American Icon'; Nancy Sinatra, *Frank Sinatra*, p7.
16   Will Friedwald, *Sinatra*, p19.

09/ Nancy: the Reagan years
1   Anthony Summers and Robbyn Swan, *Sinatra: The Life*, p350.
2   Kitty Kelley, *His Way*, p433.

3   Donald Clarke, *All Or Nothing At All: A Life of Frank Sinatra* (London, 1998), p266.
4   Donald Clarke, *All Or Nothing At All*, p270.
5   Chris Rojek, *Frank Sinatra*, p52.
6   Lawrence J Quirk and William Schoell, *The Rat Pack*, p314.
7   *Los Angeles Times*, 4 July 1991.

Frank Sinatra discography

There are hundreds of Sinatra albums available in every high street record shop – so where do you start? A good place is with one of the numerous Sinatra greatest hits packages. One of the best and cheapest is *My Way: The Best Of Frank Sinatra*. If you want to hear Sinatra's 1940s recordings of 'The House I Live In', 'Ol' Man River' and 'Nancy', there is a great compilation album called *Frank Sinatra Romance*. Also available are the fantastic box sets of Sinatra's early years, Capitol years and Reprise years – but I warn you, they are expensive.

But there is a problem with Sinatra compilation albums – they don't do the singer justice. The greatest Sinatra albums, from the 1950s and early 1960s, create a mood and feeling and are best played as a whole. So I have made a short list of what are, in my opinion, some of his greatest albums.

Songs For Swingin' Lovers Regarded by many as Sinatra's greatest album. You know all the songs – 'I've Got You Under My Skin', 'You Make Me Feel So Young', 'Old Devil Moon', 'Anything Goes'… Essential.

In The Wee Small Hours Recorded as Sinatra's marriage to Ava Gardner was falling apart, it is a melancholic study of sadness and loneliness – a masterpiece. Three other albums which capture Sinatra at his lonesome best are **No One Cares**, **Only The Lonely** and **Where Are You?**

A Swingin' Affair It does just what the title says – it swings like a monkey. If you like your music upbeat and optimistic, this is the album for you.

Come Fly With Me / Come Dance With Me / Come Swing With Me Billy May produced these albums, which display all the exuberance and hope of the 1950s.

The Concert Sinatra Recorded with a 60-piece orchestra at the same time as the Civil Rights Movement was marching in Birmingham, Alabama, Sinatra looks back at his past catalogue. The full meaning of Sinatra's stunning recordings of 'Ol' Man River' and 'Lost In The Stars' were not lost on Martin Luther King.

Sinatra At The Sands The third and final Sinatra-Basie collaboration. This one lives up to all expectations. Atomic brass from the band and Sinatra in fine voice – what a combination. There are brilliant versions of 'Come Fly With Me', 'Angel Eyes', 'Fly Me To The Moon' and 'One For My Baby'.

John Coltrane

JAZZ, RACISM AND RESISTANCE

Martin Smith

■ I was an active participant in many of the events Martin writes about. This excellent book makes me think about many of them in a different way! I'm not sure I agree with everything Martin says – but that is the point of this book. It is meant to challenge our perceptions of music and the Civil Rights Movement. I believe the same spirit can be found in the music of John Coltrane. I recommend this book to both radicals and music fans alike.

– McCoy Tyner, June 2003

Shakespeare
IN HIS TIMES FOR OUR TIMES

Michael Rosen

■ When anyone produces a Shakespeare for their time they usually reduce him to their own lack of vision. Mike Rosen is different. He places Shakespeare firmly in his own time – and so makes him belong even more to our time. His Shakespeare is disturbed, demanding, angry, astonishingly radical and human enough even to sometimes be frightened. The problems he struggled with come to a head in our world. Mike Rosen writes of him with great insight and generosity, and never belittles him. But for him Shakespeare is not just a sage wandering around the horizon, but someone you could bump into any time coming round the street corner. Yet in the end my respect and awe for Shakespeare were even greater, and so was my understanding. I wish I'd read this book years ago. It's as if Mike Rosen pointed to someone standing at his elbow and said, 'Meet your contemporary Shakespeare!' Uncannily, I think I did.
– Edward Bond, playwright and theatre director

■ A concise, unapologetically, political argument for a more dangerous Shakespeare.
– Adriano Shaplin, The Riot Group and author of *Pugilist Specialist*

Blake

THE SCOURGE OF TYRANTS

Judy Cox

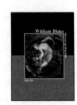

■ Judy Cox has written a wonderfully inspiring little book about Blake. She cuts away all the romantic and reactionary drivel about him and reveals him as a prophet of liberation – political, artistic and sexual liberation. She sets him in his time as a creature of the French revolutionary fervour, and expertly distinguishes him from the other great poets and writers of the Enlightenment. Quite impossible to miss.
– Paul Foot, writer and author of *Red Shelley*

■ Judy Cox's study of Blake challenges those critics who have tried to take Blake's work out of its political context – critics who would deny that 'Tyger' is a great poem about revolution.
– Tom Paulin, writer, poet and author of *The Invasion Handbook*

bookmarks the socialist bookshop

for all your anti-war and anti-capitalist books

    plus

- classic and contemporary Marxism
- trade union resources and British labour history
- radical fiction, culture and an excellent children's section
- videos, audio CDs and political journals, together with a
  well stocked second hand section
- and much more from black struggle to Irish history

- full mail order service from
  Bookmarks
  1 Bloomsbury Street, London WC1B 3QE
  020 7637 1848
  www.bookmarks.uk.com